# Whitby Ontario Book 2 in Colour Photos, Saving Our History One Photo at a Time

Photography
by Barbara Raué
2018

Series Name: Cruising Ontario

Book 202: Whitby Book 2

Cover photo: 21 Princess Street, Page 37

# Series Name: Cruising Ontario
## Saving Our History One Photo at a Time
## in colour photos

Books Available in Alphabetical Order:
Aberfoyle, Acton, Alton, Amherstburg, Ancaster, Arthur, Auburn, Aylmer, Ayr, Beaver Valley, Belgrave, Belleville, Bloomingdale, Blyth, Brantford, Brockville, Burford, Burlington, Caledon, Caledonia, Cambridge, Carlow, Chatsworth, Clifford, Collingwood, Conestogo, Delhi, Dorchester to Aylmer, Drayton, Drumbo, Dundas, Dunlop, Eden Mills, Elmira, Elora, Erin, Essex, Fergus, Goderich, Grimsby, Guelph, Hagersville, Hamilton, Hanover, Harriston, Hespeler, Jarvis, Kingston, Kingsville, Kitchener, Lake Superior, Lincoln, Linwood, Listowel, London, Lucknow, Merrickville, Mono, Mount Forest, Mount Pleasant, Neustadt, New Hamburg, Newboro, Newport, Niagara-on-the-Lake, Oakville, Onondaga, Orangeville, Orillia, Owen Sound, Palmerston, Paris, Pelham, Perth, Peterborough, Petrolia, Port Colborne, Port Elgin, Portland, Preston, Rockwood, Sarnia, Sault Ste. Marie, Seaforth, Sheffield, Shelburne, Simcoe, Smiths Falls, Smithville, Southampton, St. Catharines, St. George, St. Jacobs, St. Marys, St. Thomas, Stoney Creek, Stratford, Thamesford, Thunder Bay, Tillsonburg, Toronto, Waterdown, Waterford, Waterloo, Welland, Wellesley, West Flamborough, Westport, Whitby, Windsor, Wingham, Woodstock

Book 198: Chatsworth
Book 199: Wingham
Book 200: West Flamborough
Book 201-202: Whitby

# Other Books by Barbara Raue

Coins of Gold

Arrows, Indians and Love

The Life and Times of Barbara
Volume 1: Inventions That Have Enhanced My Life
Volume 2: Entertainment That I Have Enjoyed
Volume 3: East Coast Trips
Volume 4: Olympics Have Always Intrigued Me
Volume 5: Wonders of the World
Volume 6: Caribbean Cruises We Have Enjoyed
Volume 7: Animals
Volume 8: Storms and Other Major Disasters in My Lifetime
Volume 9: Wars, Terrorist Attacks and Major Disasters

The Cromwell Family Book

Laura Secord Discovered

Daddy Where Are You?

Montana Series
Book 1: Montana Dream
Book 2: Life on the Montana Frontier
Book 3: Montana to Boston and Back
Book 4: Montana Sons Go to War
Book 5: Montana Sons Return from War

Visit Barbara's website to view all of her books
http://barbararaue.ca

## Table of Contents

Brooklin

| | |
|---|---|
| Baldwin Street | Page 6 |
| Cassels Road West | Page 22 |
| Cassels Road East | Page 23 |
| Pitt Street | Page 32 |
| Princess Street | Page 33 |
| Colston Avenue | Page 40 |
| George Street | Page 41 |
| Queen Street | Page 42 |
| Duke Street | Page 42 |

Port Whitby

| | |
|---|---|
| Victoria Street East | Page 44 |
| Dufferin Street | Page 45 |
| Front Street | Page 50 |
| Brock Street South | Page 51 |
| Watson Street West | Page 53 |
| Henry Street | Page 54 |

©All the photos in this book have been taken with my cameras. I own the rights to them. I confirm that I have not submitted any content for which I do not have the exclusive publishing rights. I adhere to all terms in the Content Guidelines when publishing new content.

First Nations people were the original inhabitants of the area that would become Brooklin. In the 1820s European pioneers established a small settlement in the area. The settlement expanded in the 1840s when brothers John and Robert Campbell established a flour mill on Lynde Creek. Most of the buildings in the area of the walking tour are single-detached houses. It is a diverse collection of traditional architectural styles from the mid-nineteenth to mid-twentieth centuries. These diverse styles complement the landscape as the spaces between buildings offer glimpses of the creek, small parks, and treed open spaces.

In 1819, John Scadding, clerk for Lieutenant-Governor John Graves Simcoe, was awarded a large tract of land now known as Port Whitby. Originally known as Port Windsor, the area encompassed the natural harbour in the south up to Victoria Street in the north. Soon after settlement, the harbour was used to ship local grain, lumber, and farm produce across Canada and the United States. Farmers transported their produce to Port Windsor using a plank toll road, now Brock Street, and the Port Whitby, Port Perry, and Lindsay Railway. From the 1840s to the 1870s, Windsor Harbour prospered, leading to a number of developments that modernized the harbour's infrastructure and surrounding industry. It was also during this time, in 1847, that Windsor Harbour was officially renamed Whitby Harbour. The bustling community of Port Whitby sprung up around the harbour with a number of houses, hotels, shops, and breweries supporting further development. Port Whitby, including the harbour, was one of three communities that formed the original Town of Whitby in 1855 along with Hamer's Corners and Perry's Corners.

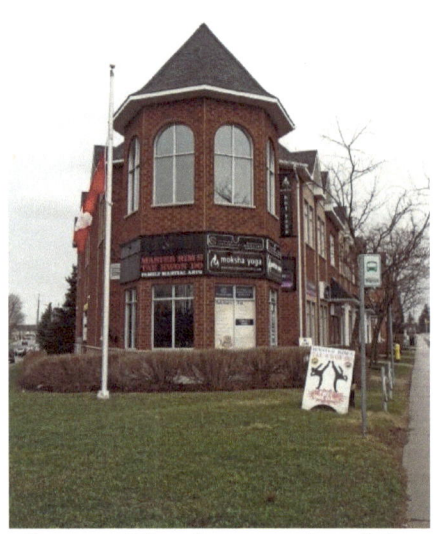

31 Baldwin Street - Newly completed 2 storey frame commercial building with a triangular shape, brick cladding, gable roof with dormers, hexagonal tower

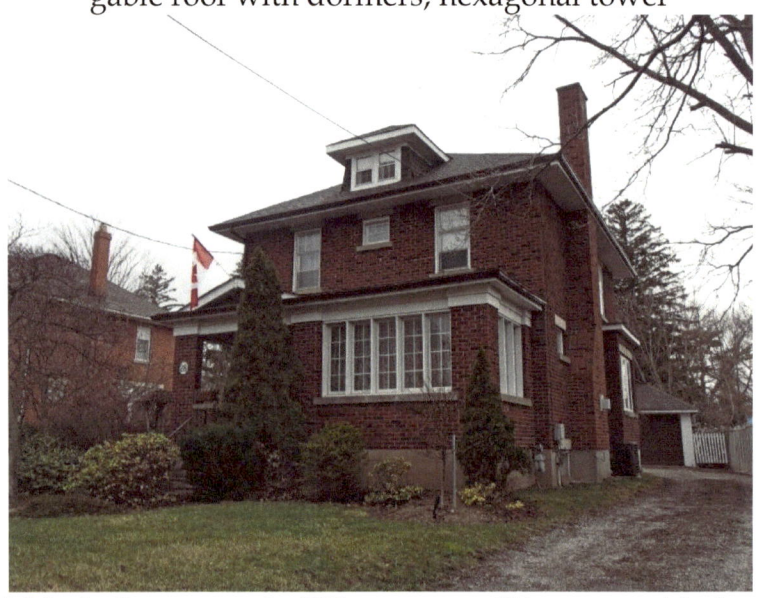

28 Baldwin Street – early 20th century – 2½ storey with dormer in hip roof

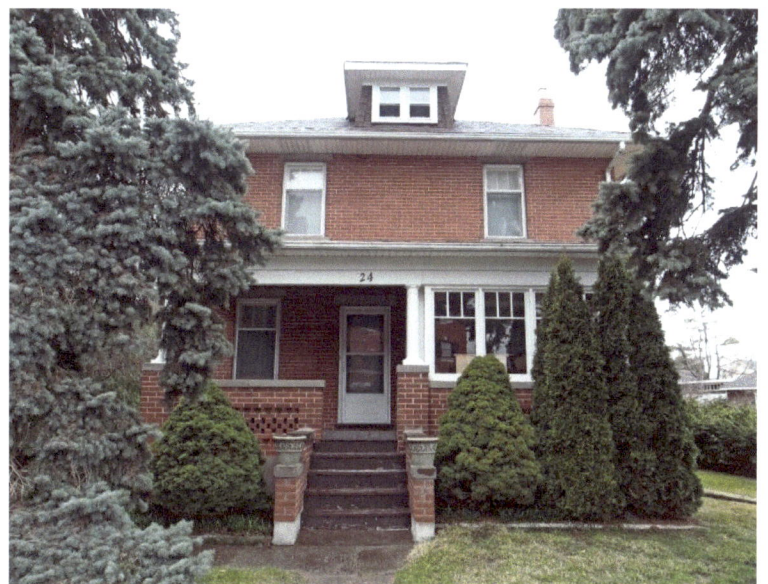

24 Baldwin Street – early 20th century – 2½ storey with brick cladding; partially enclosed full-width porch

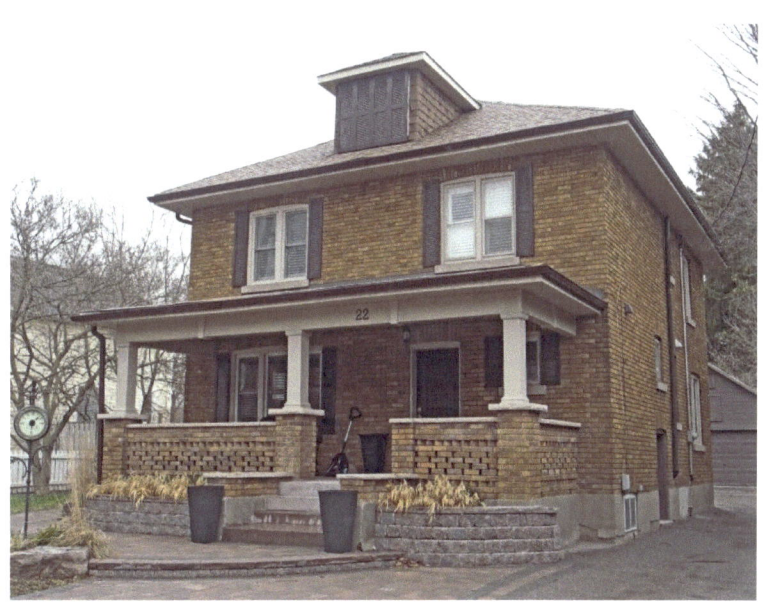

22 Baldwin Street – early 20th century – 2½ storey, Edwardian Classic style, hip roof with gabled dormer

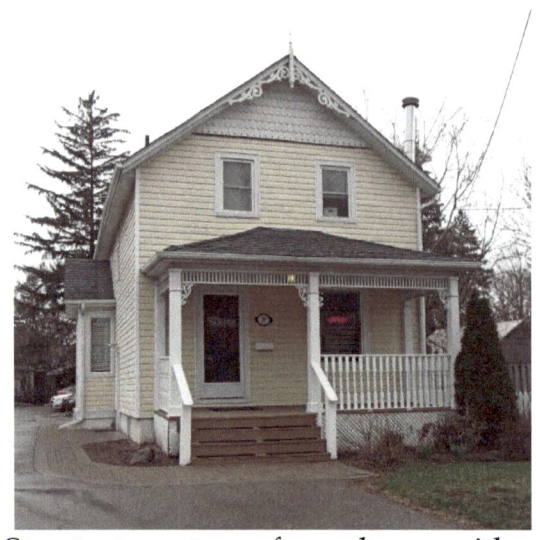

20 Baldwin Street – two-storey frame house with gable to front with barge board and finial; offset entrance and full width porch

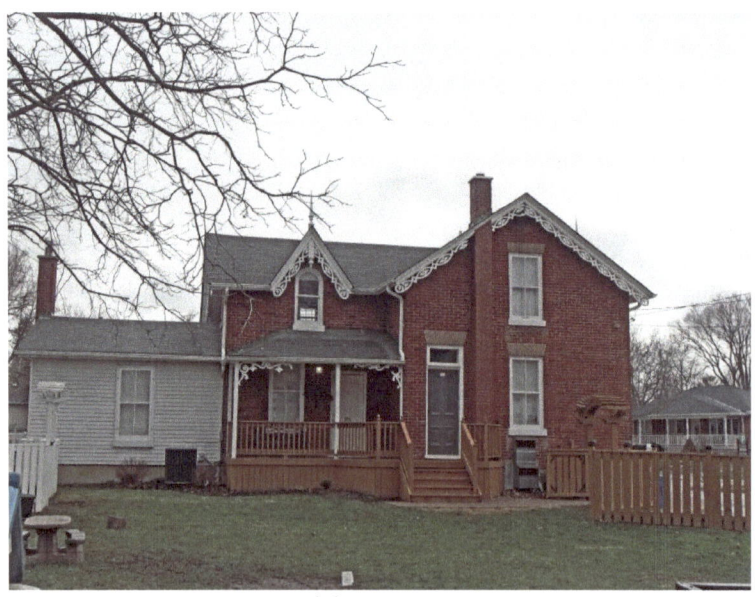

Baldwin Street

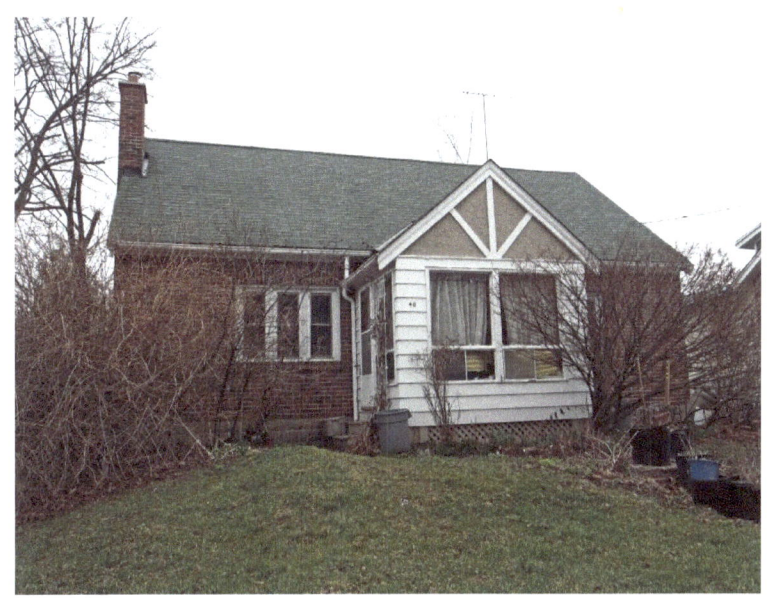

40 Baldwin Street – early to mid-20th century

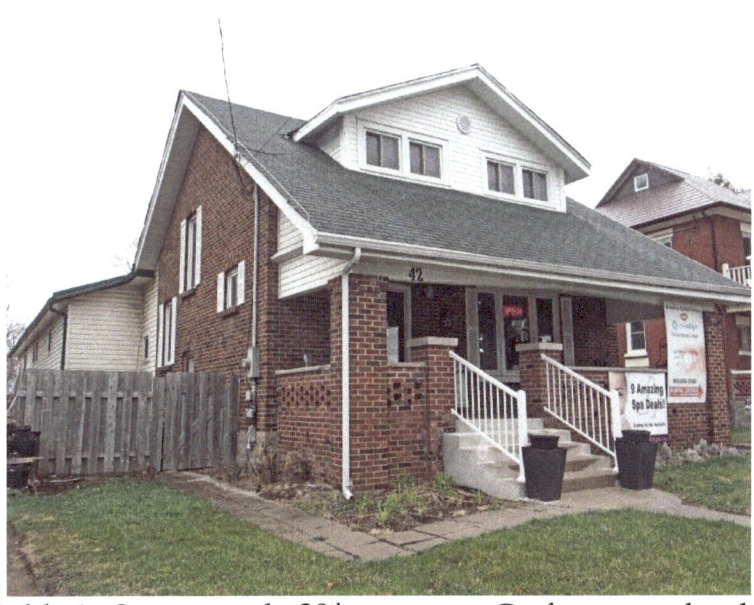

42 Baldwin Street – early 20th century – Craftsman style – large gable roof overhanging a full-width porch with an engaged gabled dormer

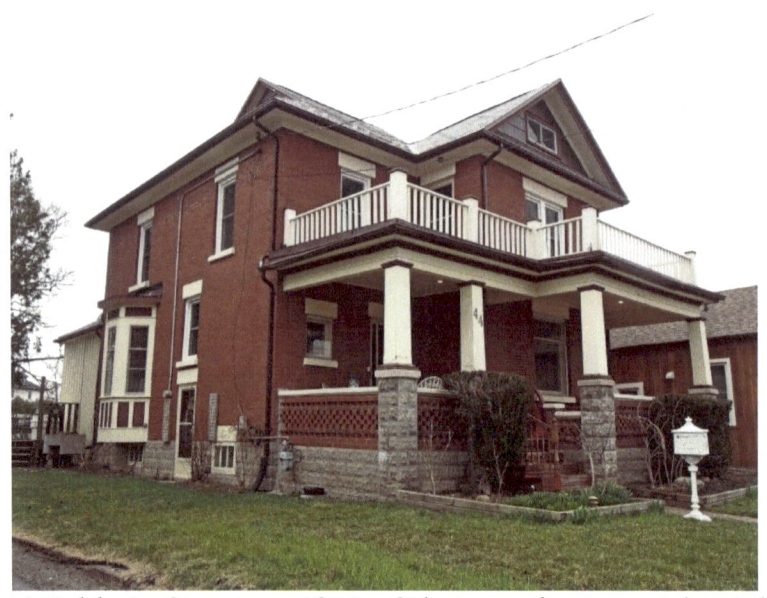

44 Baldwin Street - c. 1914 – 2½ storey frame residential building in the Edwardian Classic style, brick cladding, hip gable roof, L-shape with a wing projecting from the main block gable end to the street, a flat-roofed verandah with open porch above

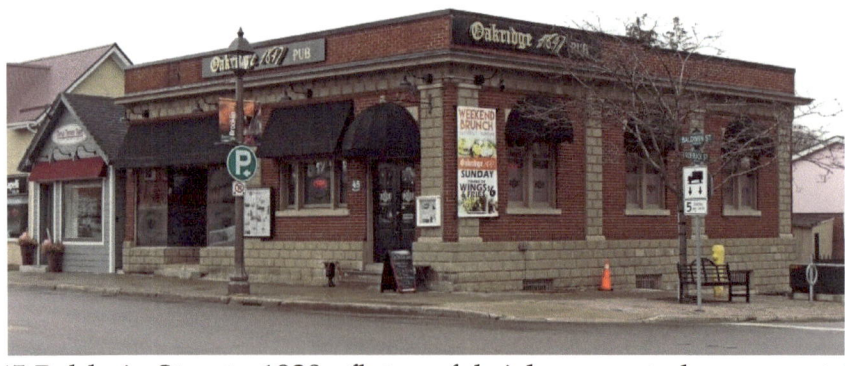

45 Baldwin Street - 1929 - flat roof, brick parapet above a metal cornice, a two bay façade, concrete block pilasters flanking each bay, double and triple windows on each face with concrete lintels and sills

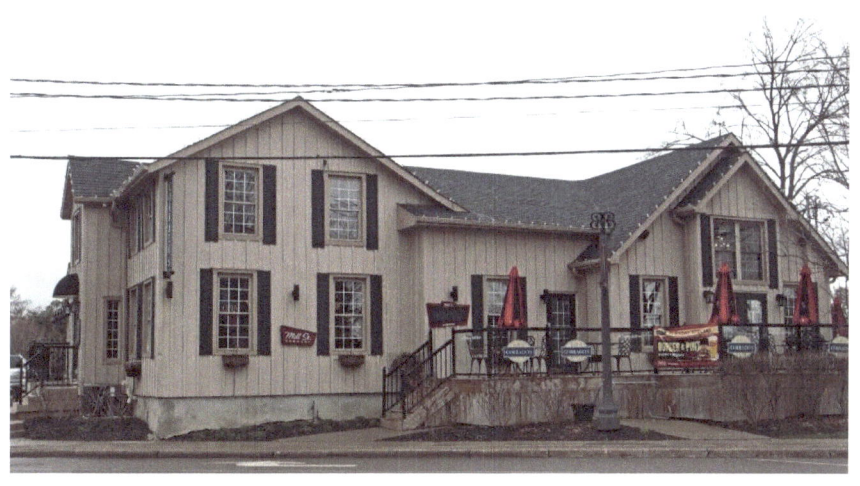

38 Baldwin Street – Corrado's Restaurant and Bar

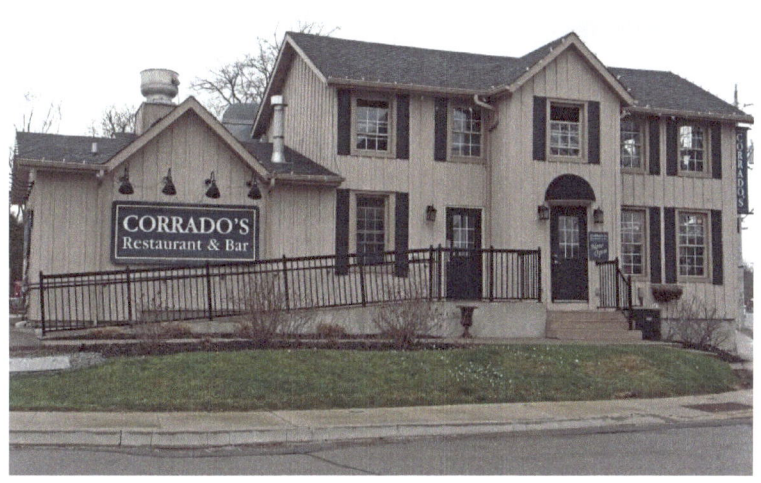

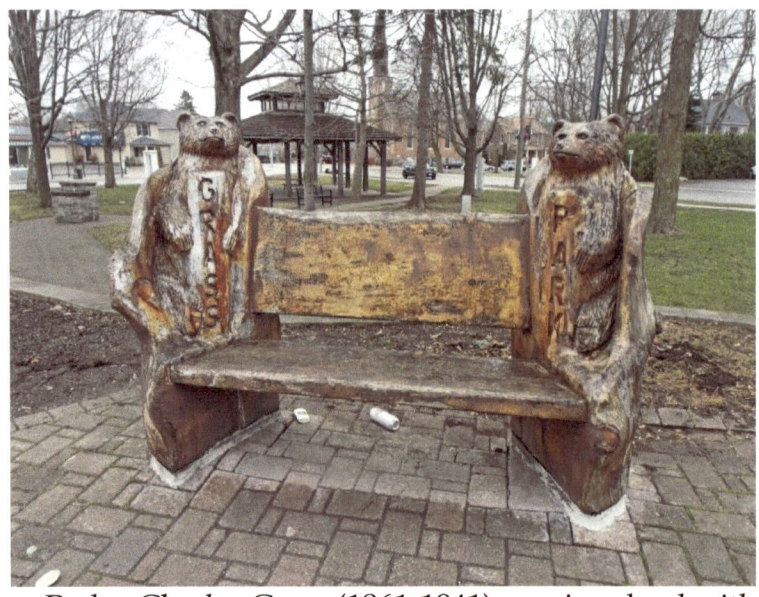

Grass Park – Charles Grass (1861-1941) was involved with the Brooklin Mill. After the fire of 1865, he acquired this site and maintained it as a park.

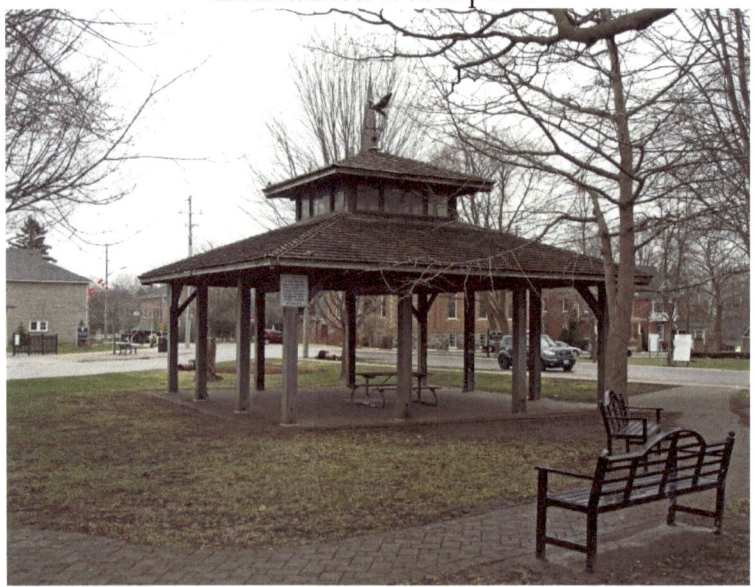

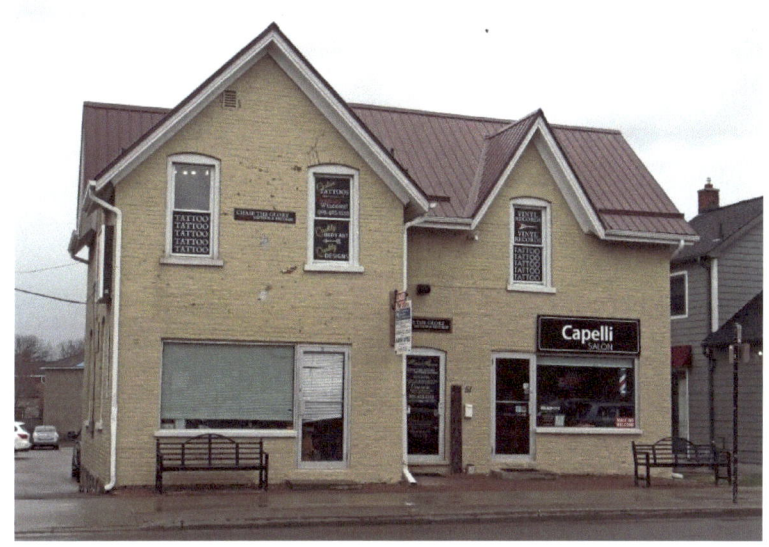

51 Baldwin Street - c. 1897 – 2½ storey brick, gable roofed commercial building with a gable centred in the main block and a projecting wing to the north, gable end to the street

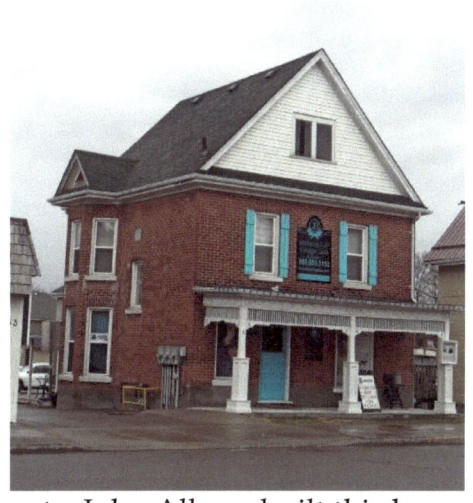

53 Baldwin Street – John Allems built this house in 1898 as his residence in Edwardian Classic style; he operated his business as harness maker from 1896-1946 in the building next door.

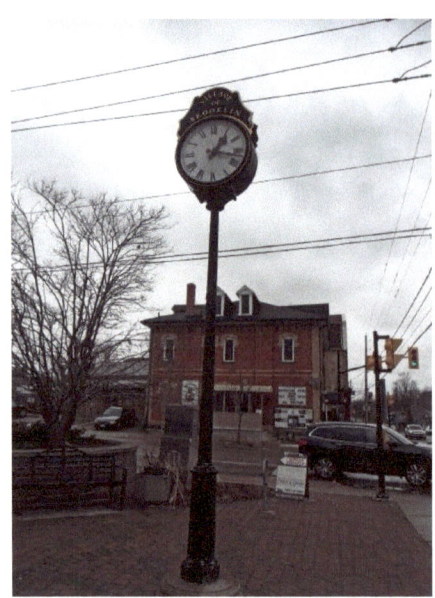

Clock

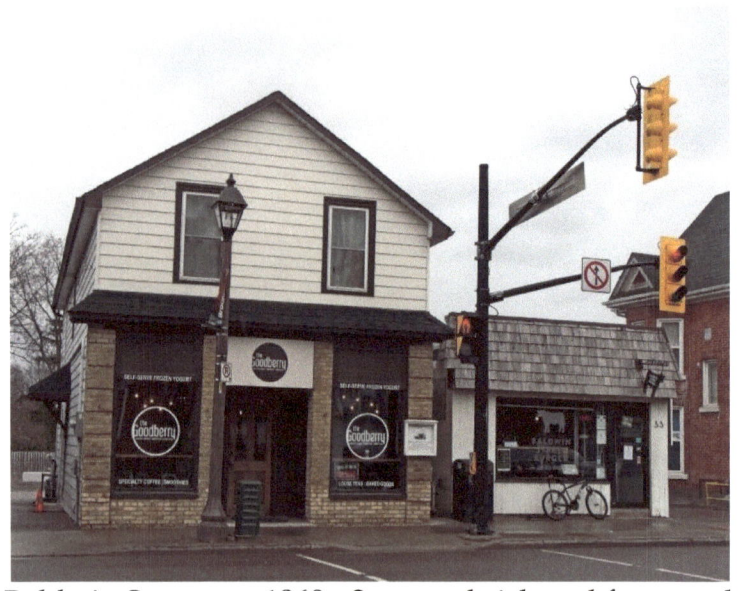

55 Baldwin Street – c. 1860 - 2 storey brick and frame gable-roofed commercial building, ribbed brick pilasters

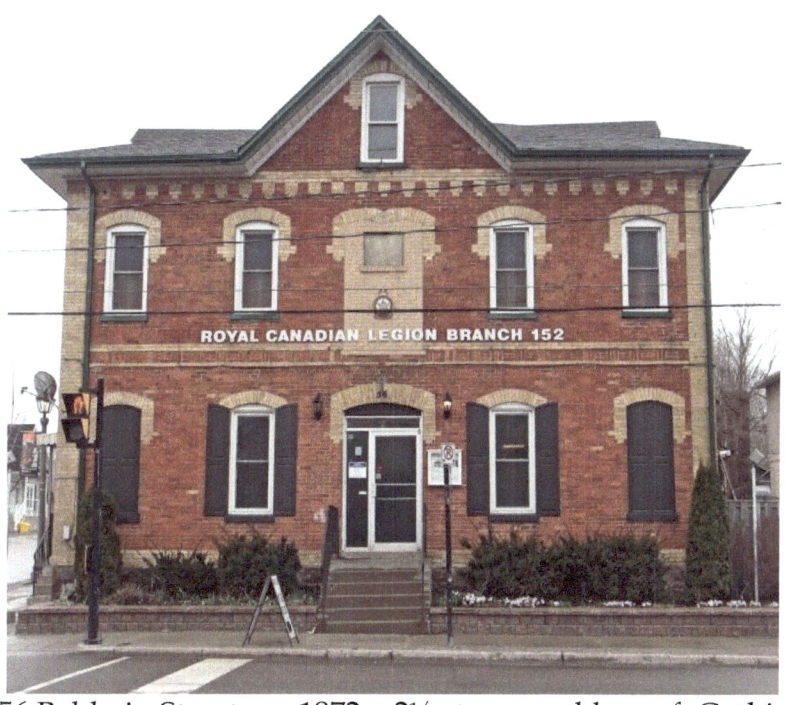

56 Baldwin Street – c. 1872 - 2½ storey, gable roof, Gothic Revival influences, decorative brick drip mouldings over windows, decorative brick band courses, foundation and pilasters at corners – Royal Canadian Legion

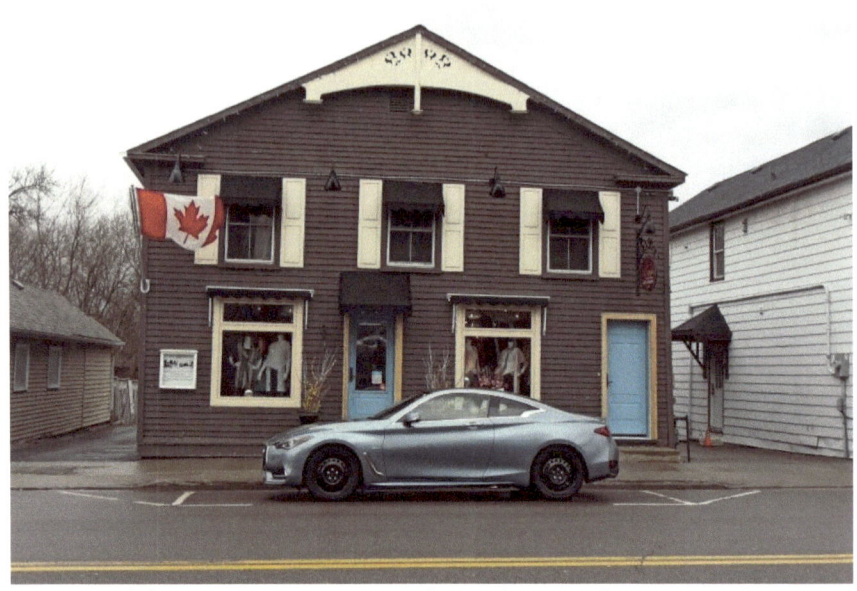

57 Baldwin Street – Connie's Ladies Fashion – c. 1847 – Classical Revival, gable roof, decorative barge boarding in the gable end, shutters on second storey windows, canvas awnings on first storey windows

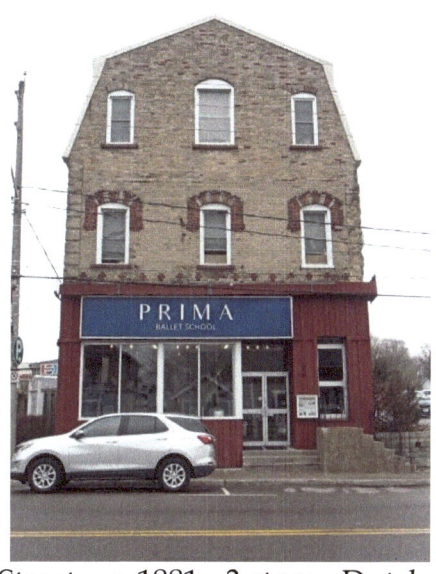

58 Baldwin Street – c. 1881 - 3 storey Dutch gabled brick commercial building with Gothic Revival influences, decorative brick drip mouldings on second storey windows, decorative brick sills, decorative brick medallions over first storey signboard

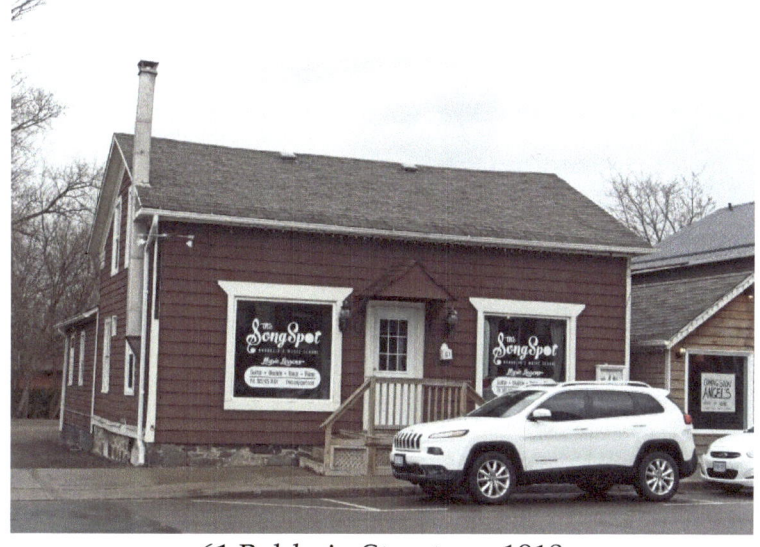

61 Baldwin Street – c. 1918

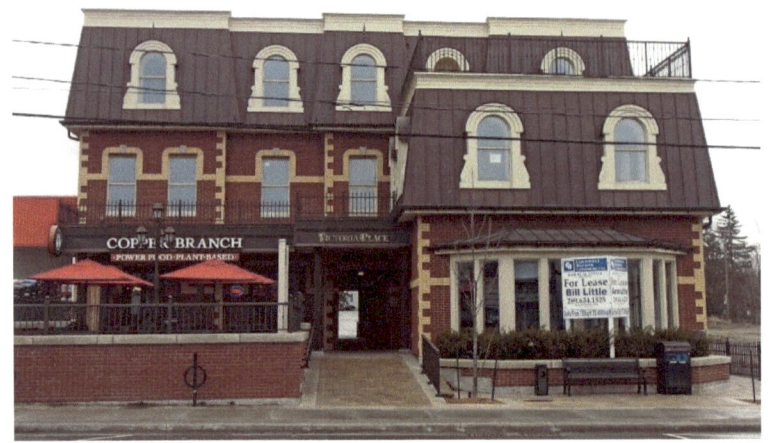

66 Baldwin Street – Victoria Place

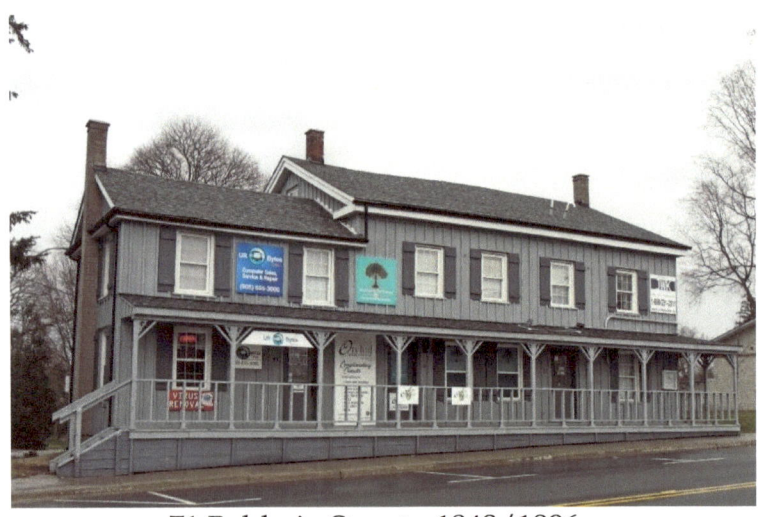

71 Baldwin Street - 1848/1896 -

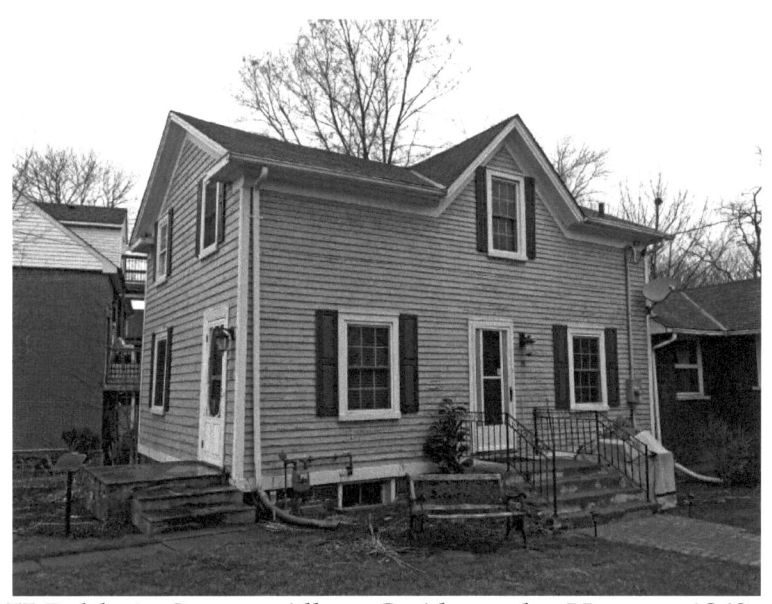

75 Baldwin Street – Albert G. Alexander House – 1863 –

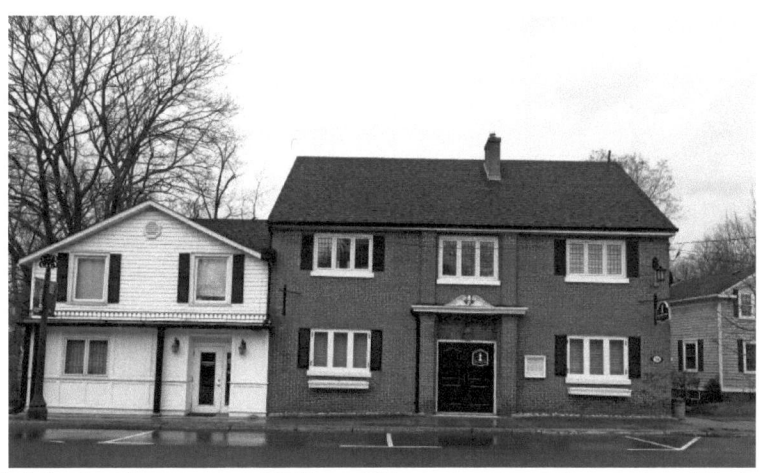

79 Baldwin Street – c. 1950s – 2½ storey, gable roof, added to a 2 storey mid-19th century frame building

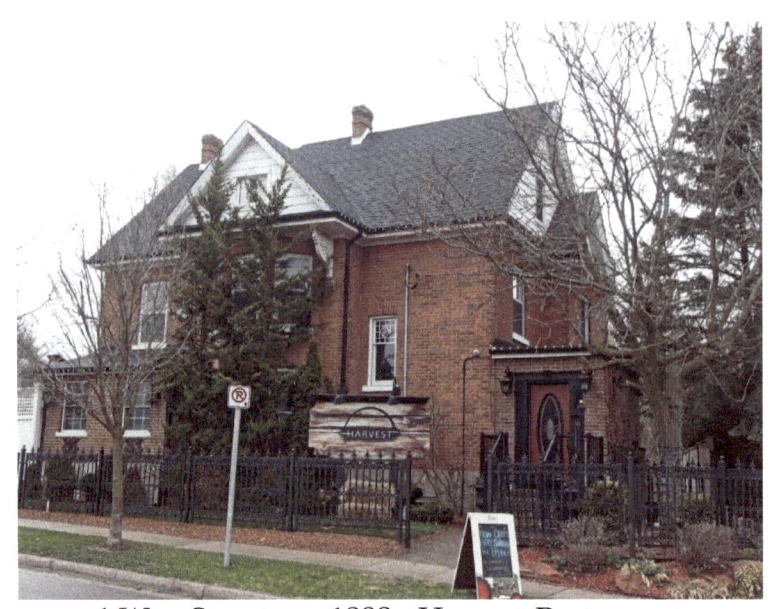

1 Way Street – c. 1898 - Harvest Restaurant

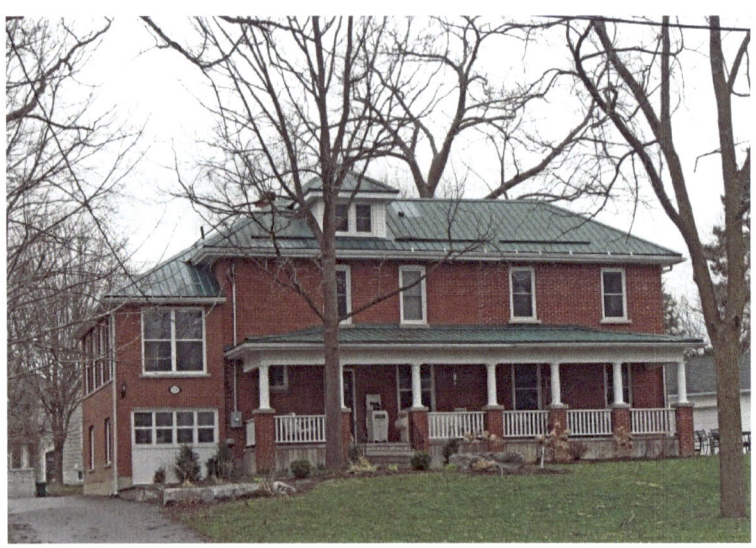

118 Baldwin Street North

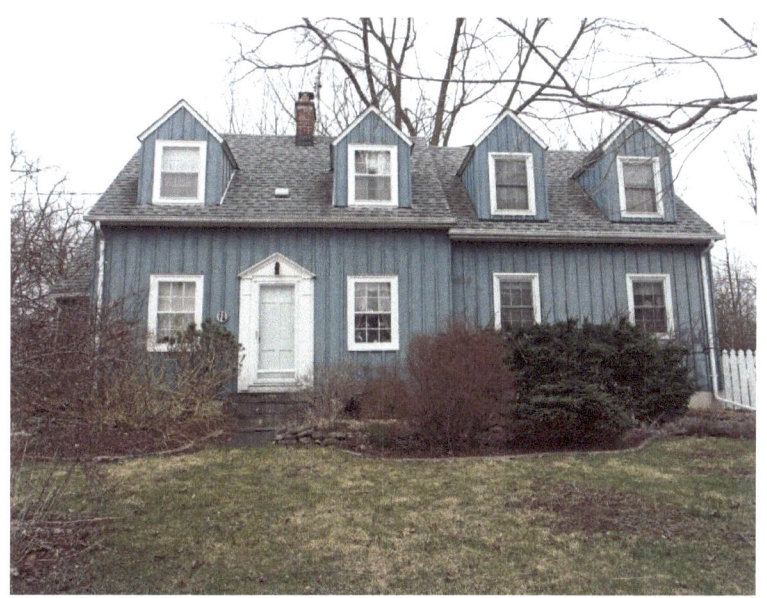

131 Baldwin Street North

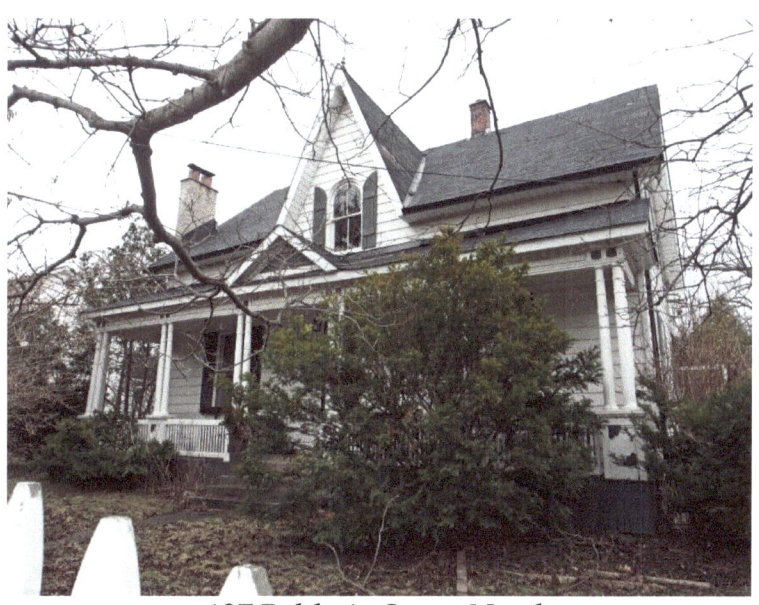

137 Baldwin Street North

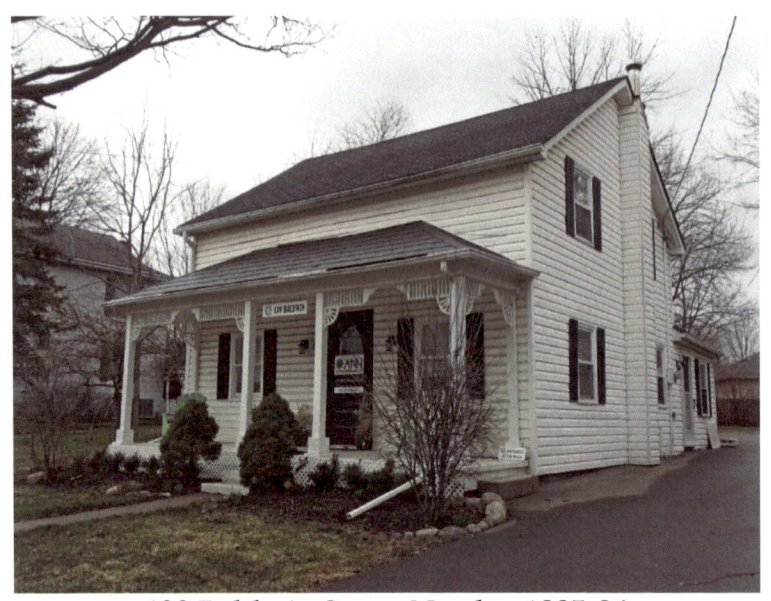

139 Baldwin Street North – 1885-86

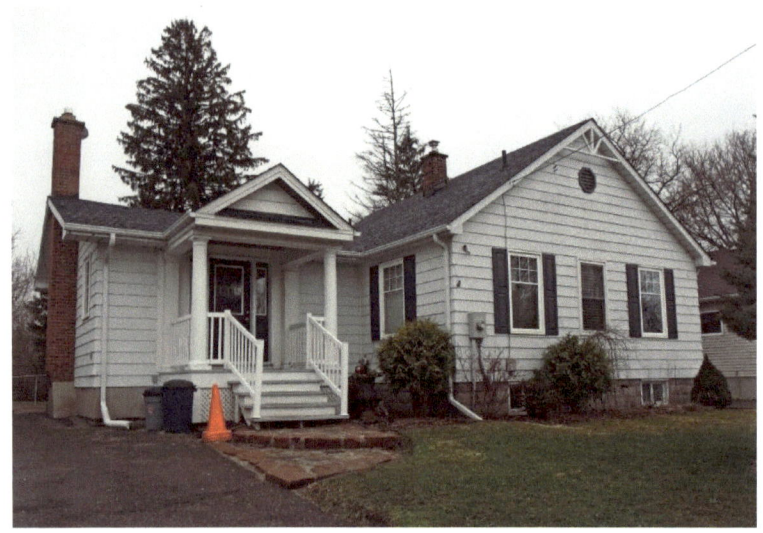

Cassels Road West

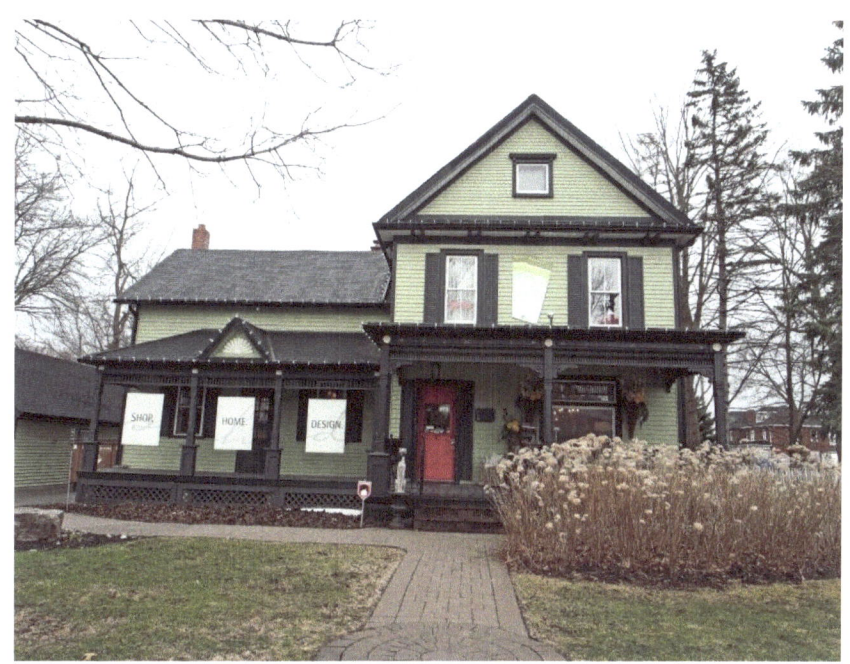

3 Cassels Road East – c. 1889 – 2½ storey frame gable roofed Victorian vernacular home was built by Charles Grass and owned by the Grass family until 1950. For many years he operated, but did not own the mill. The main block has the gable end to street, with a 1½ storey wing to the east and a projecting gable roofed bay to the west, clapboard siding, fish scale siding on gable end, decorative cornice and brackets on verandah, stained glass over first storey window.

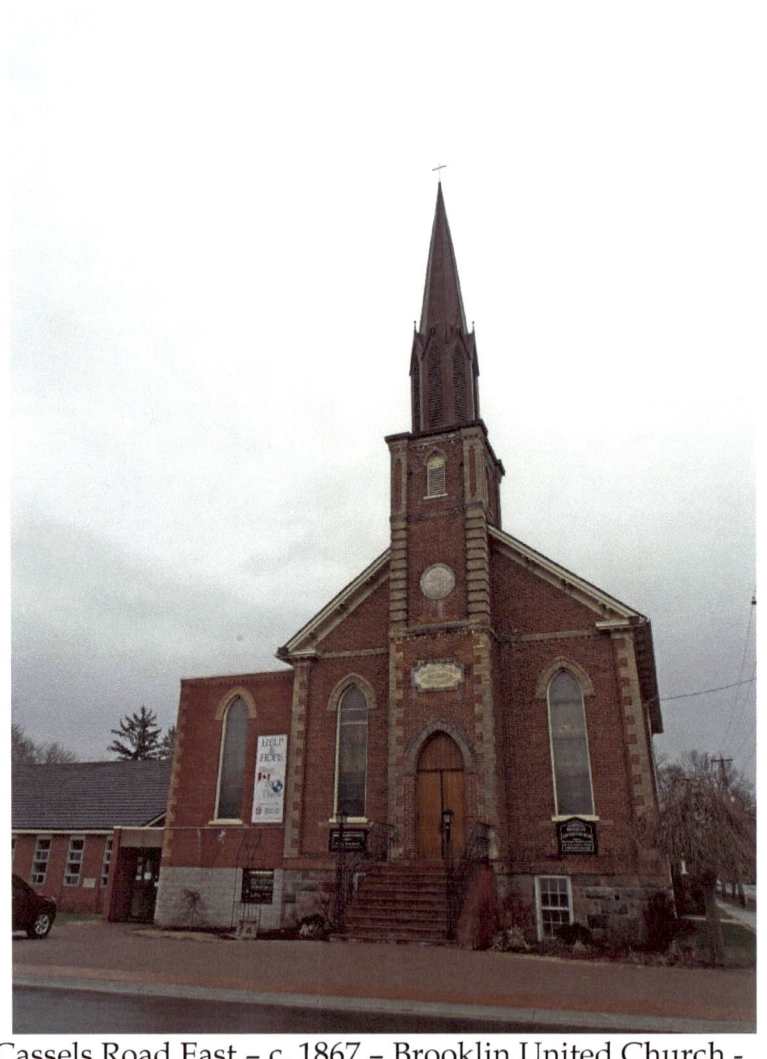

19 Cassels Road East – c. 1867 – Brooklin United Church - Gothic Revival - brick and stone tower topped with a wooden pinnacle, double height Gothic arched windows

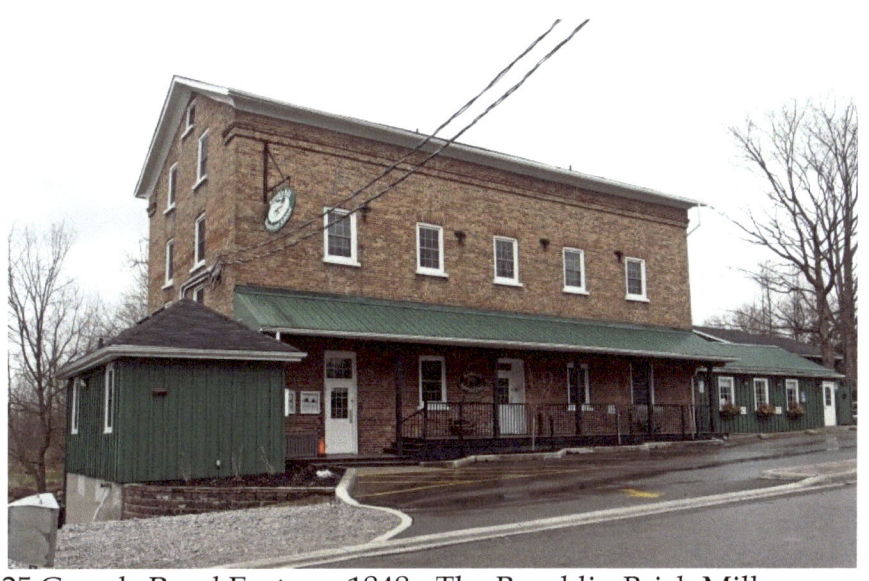

25 Cassels Road East – c. 1848 - The Brooklin Brick Mill was built for John Campbell after the original frame mill (1840) was destroyed by fire. The cedar swamp that originally covered the site was filled so that the foundation could be built on solid ground. The date is still visible on the west side gable. The mill could produce 50 barrels of flour a day and operated as a flour mill for 149 years, ceasing operation in 1991.

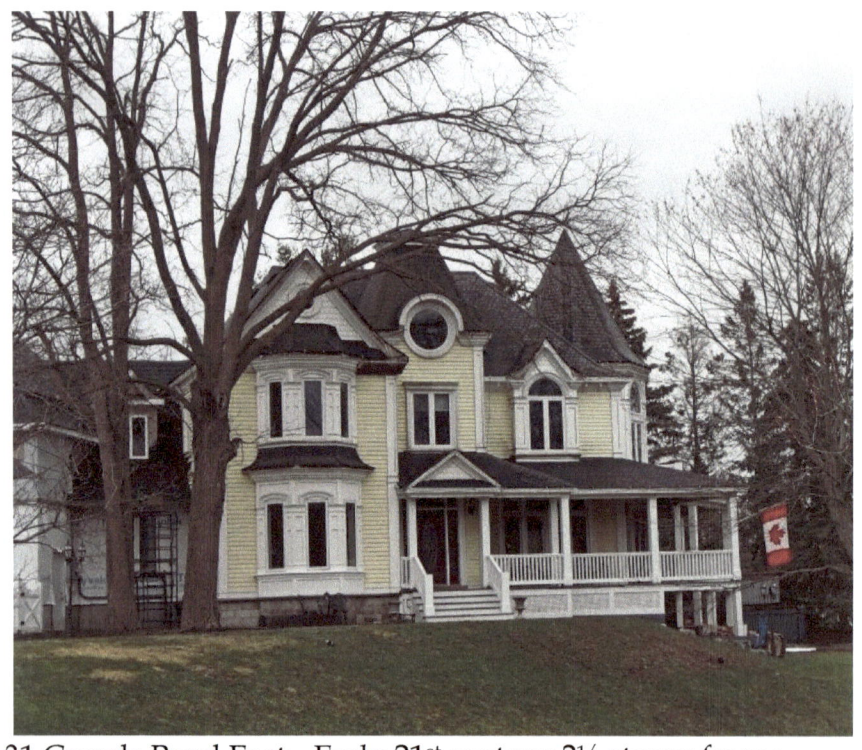

31 Cassels Road East - Early 21st century 2½ storey frame complex gable roofed residential building with eclectic late 19th century stylistic influences (mansarded central bay, turreted and gabled side bays, projecting bay windows, Palladian windows

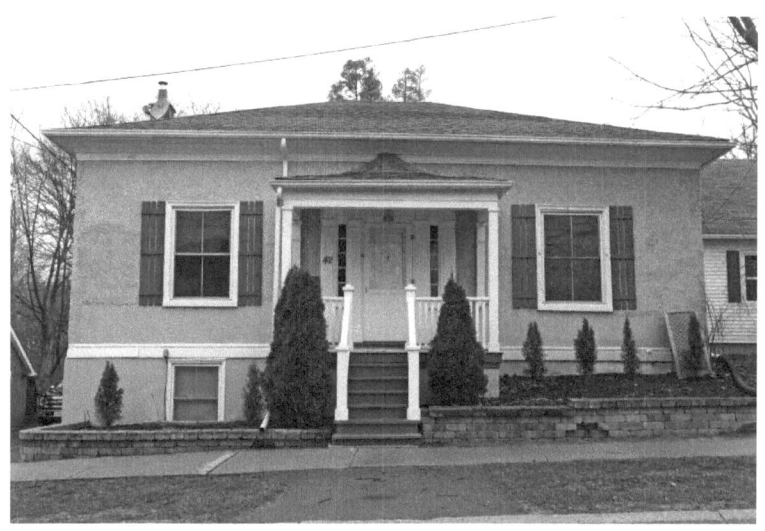

42 Cassels Road East – c. 1845 – 1½ storey Regency Cottage - simple roofline, and bell-cast porch - built by Dr. James Hunter and later sold to his son-in-law Rev. Robert Darlington. It served as a Post Office until 1881.

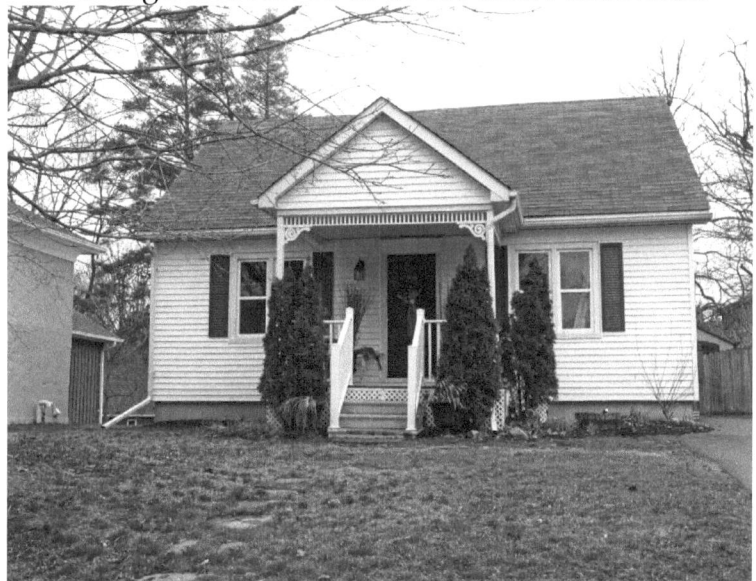

44 Cassels Road East - Mid-20th century 1½ storey frame residential building with a central entranceway under a gable roofed porch flanked by two double windows

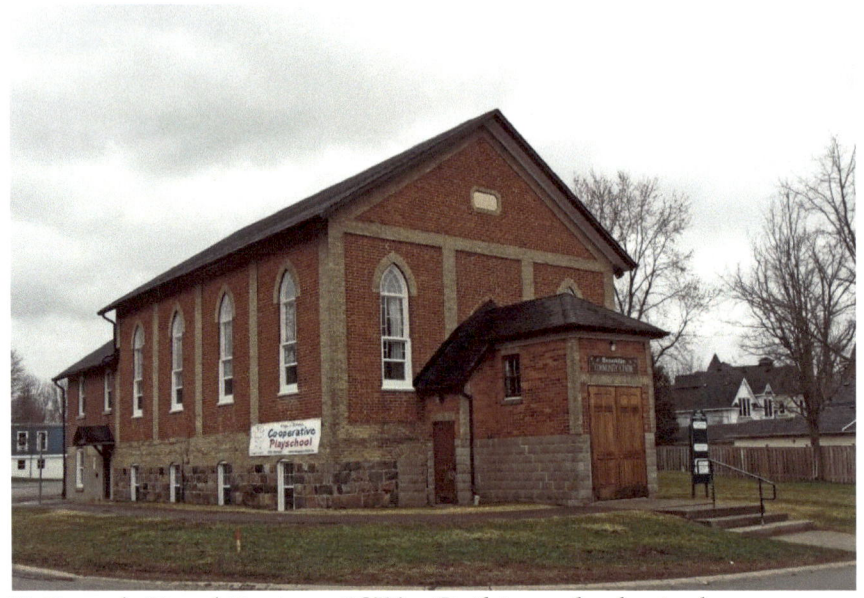

45 Cassels Road East - c. 1876 - Gothic-arched windows, decorative brick outlining around each of the three bays and around the gable end

Originally built as a Bible Christian Church, it served as a Baptist Church from 1884 until 1916. From 1920 to 1966, it was the Municipal Offices for the Township of Whitby and also served as a library during this time. It has been the Brooklin Community Centre since 1967.

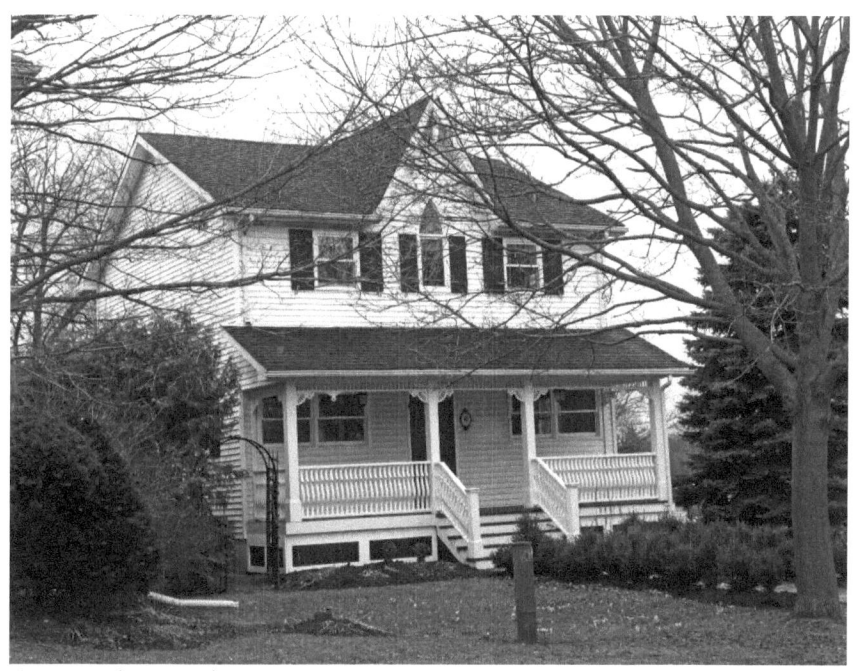

49 Cassels Road East – c. 1860s - Gothic Revival style - gable roof, central entranceway flanked by double windows under a full-width shed roofed porch with decorative railings and posts, a Gothic-arched window and matching shutters in the central gable

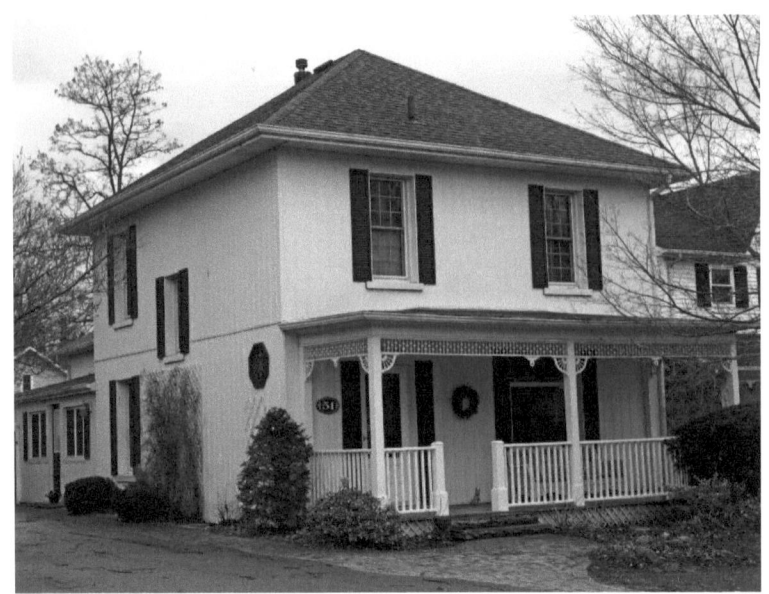

51 Cassels Road East – c. 1906 - hip roof, square plan with offset entrance next to large window under a full width shallow bell-cast roofed porch, with 9/9 windows above

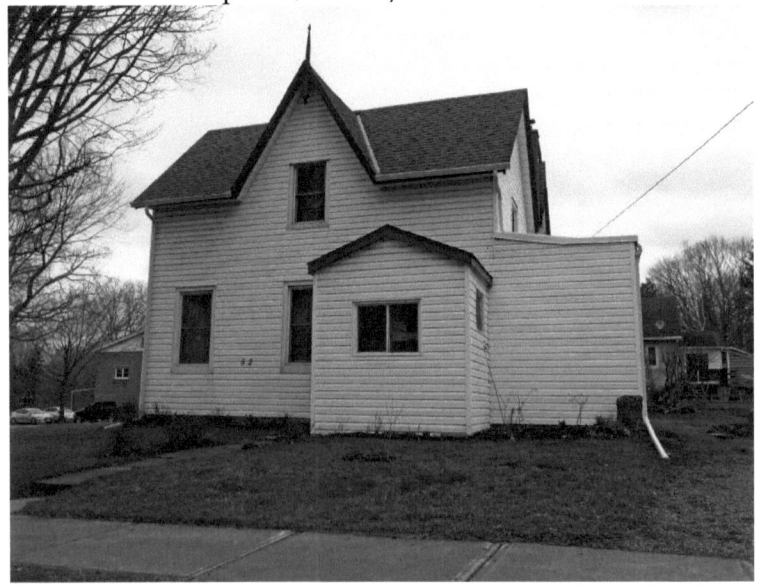

52 Cassels Road East – c. 1875 – 1½ storey gable roofed frame residential building with a central gable, an offset entrance within an enclosed vestibule

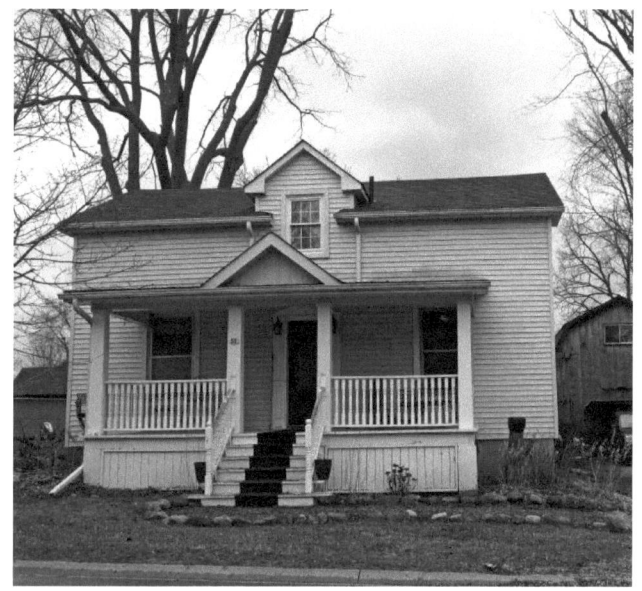

55 Cassels Road East – c. 1875

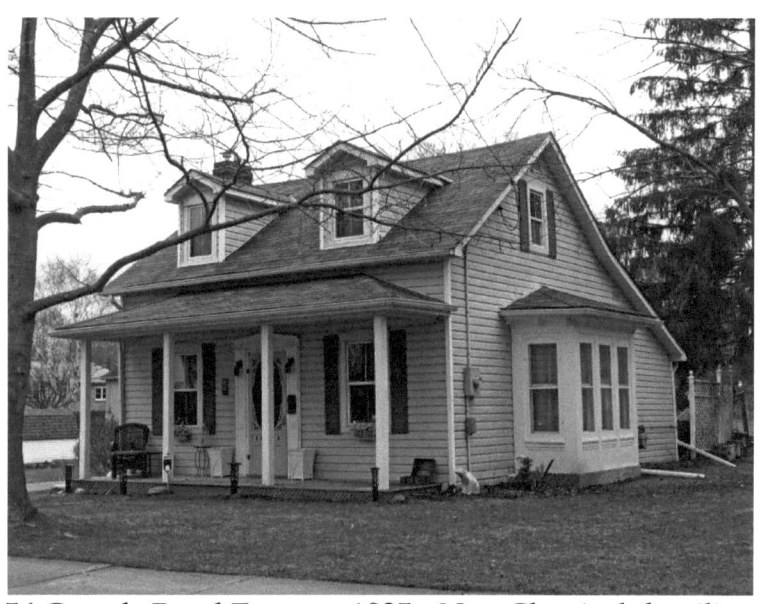

56 Cassels Road East – c. 1925 - Neo-Classical detailing

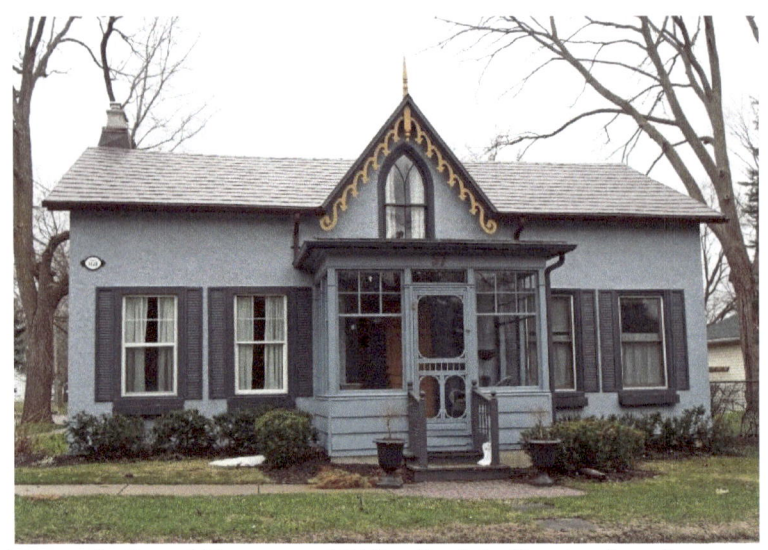

57 Cassels Road East – c. 1848 - Gothic Revival style, central entranceway within a flat roofed enclosed porch, Gothic-arched window above, decorative barge board and finial

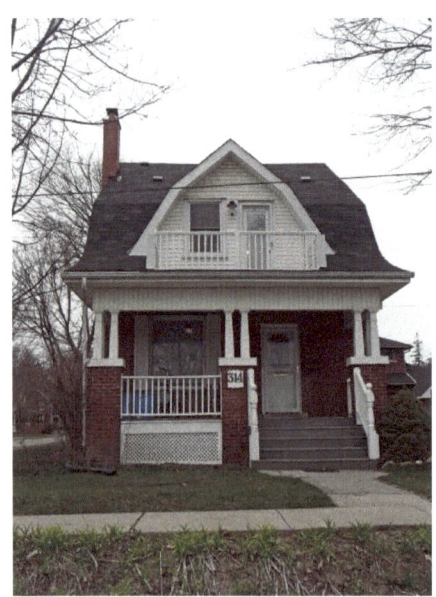

314 Pitt Street – Neo-colonial style with gambrel roof

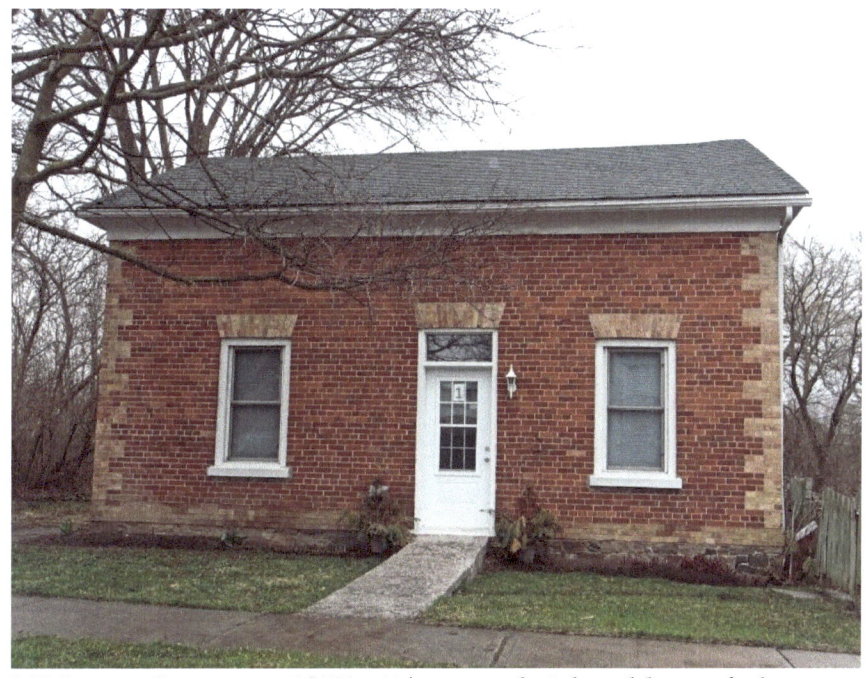

1 Princess Street – c. 1857 - 1½ storey brick gable roofed residential building, with a slightly offset central entranceway flanked by two windows, buff brick cornices on windows and door and quoins

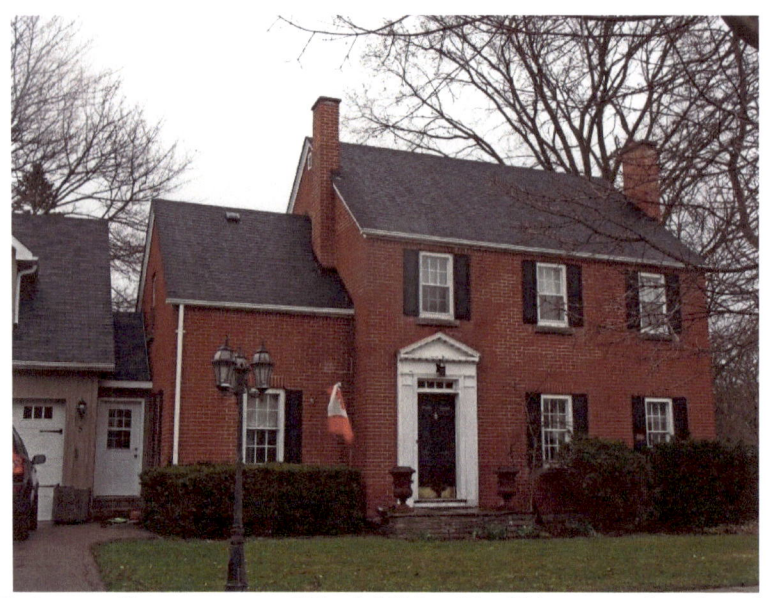

5 Princess Street – post World War II - 2½ storey brick gable roofed house – Neo-Georgian style, with a 2 storey gable roofed wing to the north

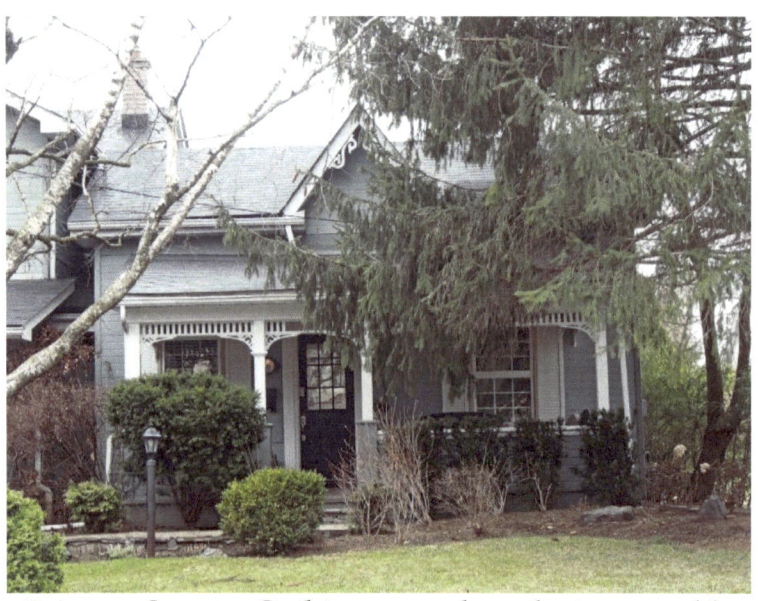

Princess Street – Gothic – verge board trim on gable

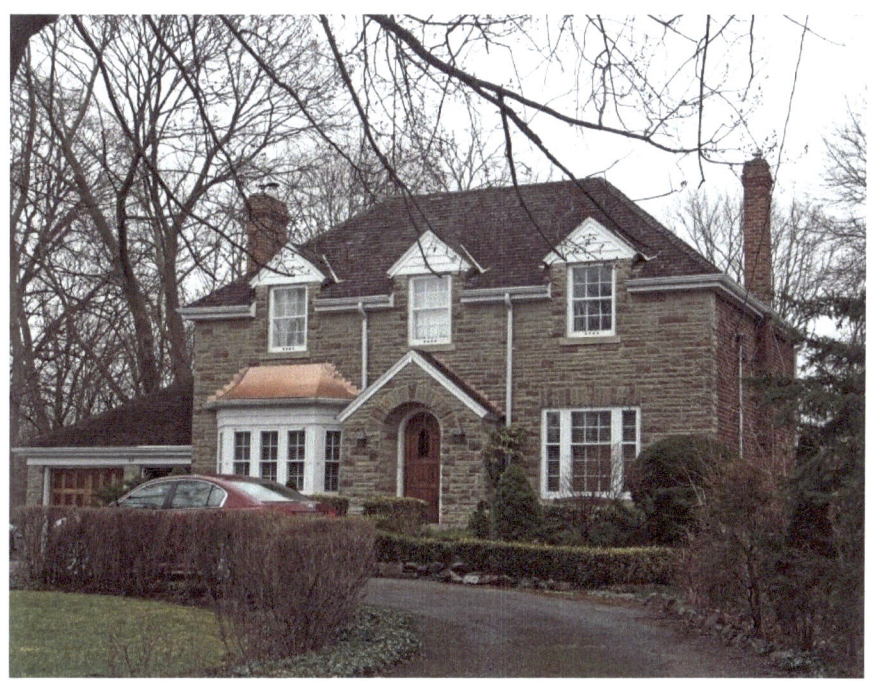

11 Princess Street – – c. 1943 - stone and brick hip gable roofed house - It has a tapestry brickwork pattern with an ashlar stone pattern (square cut building stones) on the street façade. Arthur James Cook, a Township Councillor in 1933/34, built the house after retiring from his business as a butcher shop owner.

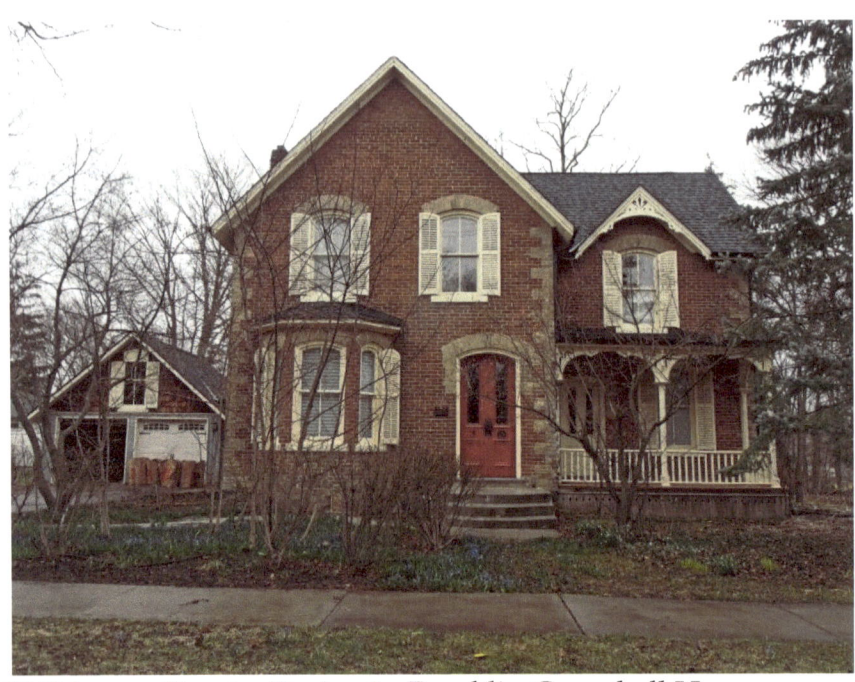

15 Princess Street – Benjamin Franklin Campbell House – c. 1877 - Gothic Revival style, large gable end block with a recessed block to the south, bay window, 2-over-2 curved top windows, ornamental white brick lintels and quoins, wooden shutters, panelled wood and glass main and secondary doors, decorative barge boarding on the porch and roof gable

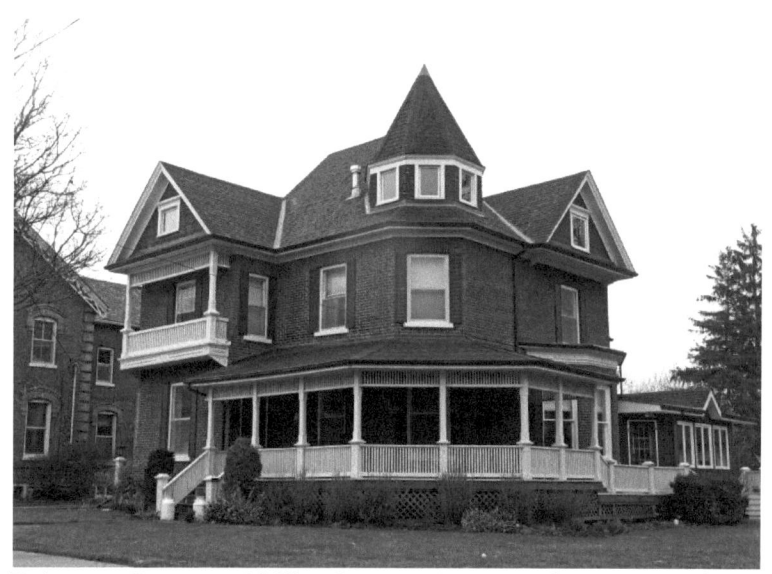

21 Princess Street – 1895 - Queen Anne style, engaged tower, chevron pattern shingles on west gable and basket weave pattern on the tower, balcony and verandah wooden railings

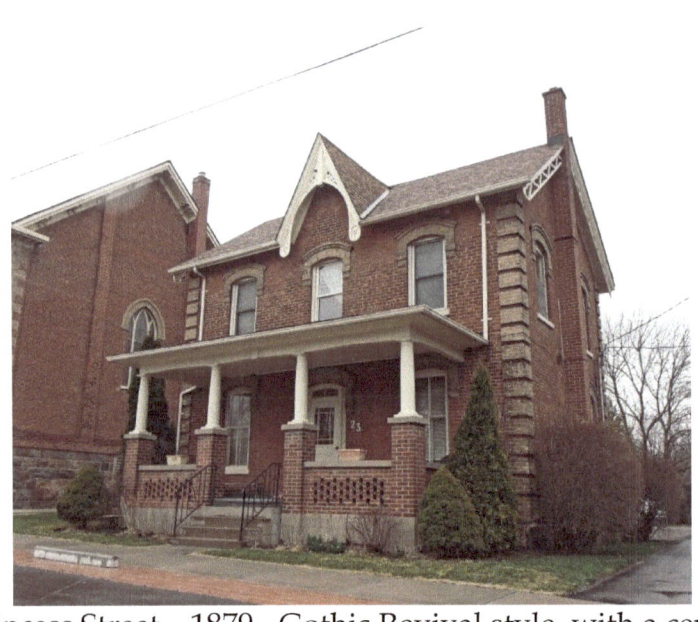

23 Princess Street – 1879 - Gothic Revival style, with a central entrance panelled wooden door with top light contained in a round-headed panelled wooden door surround with decorative brick lintel/drip moulding, flanked by two 2/2 elongated windows with similar lintels, under a shed roofed full width porch supported by turned wooden posts on brick plinths, with three similar windows in the second storey above, with the central window centred under a roof gable It was built as a Methodist parsonage by A.P. Cameron; it cost $1,700 to construct. In 1917, it became one of the first buildings to be wired for electricity in Brooklin.

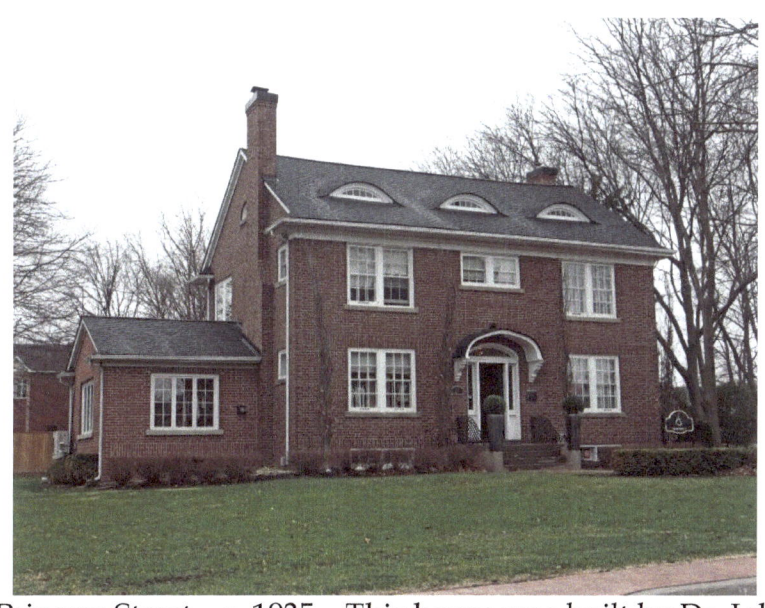

24 Princess Street – c. 1935 – This house was built by Dr. John Moore who came to Brooklin in 1891 and was a doctor here for 46 years. He was Reeve of Whitby Township from 1912-14 and served on the Brooklin School Board. The English cross bond brick pattern is rare to see and would have been expensive to produce. Central entranceway with glazed top and side lights under a slightly projecting bracketed curving wooden lintel, flanked by 6/6 double windows in the first and second storeys, with a 3/3 double window above, three eyebrow dormers with shallow windows.

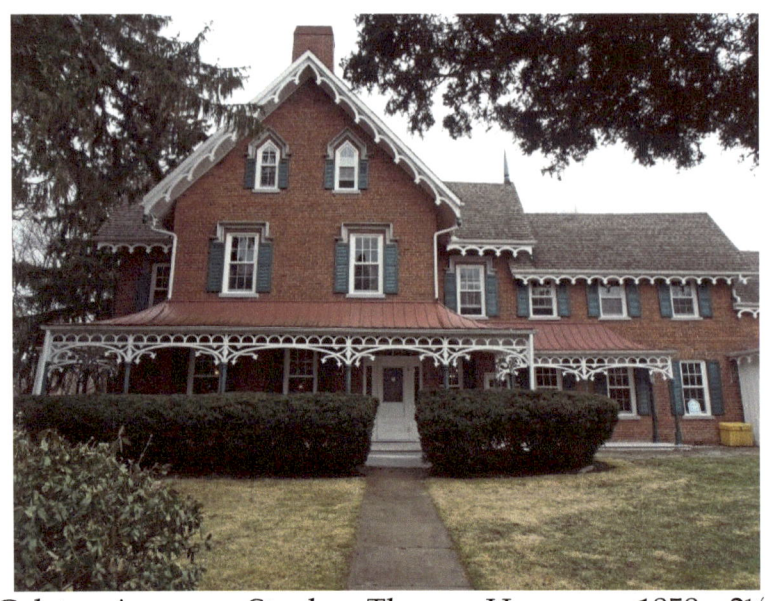

90 Colston Avenue – Stephen Thomas House – c. 1858 – 2½ storey brick gable roofed building with Gothic Revival influences - best surviving mansion and grounds from the early days of the village

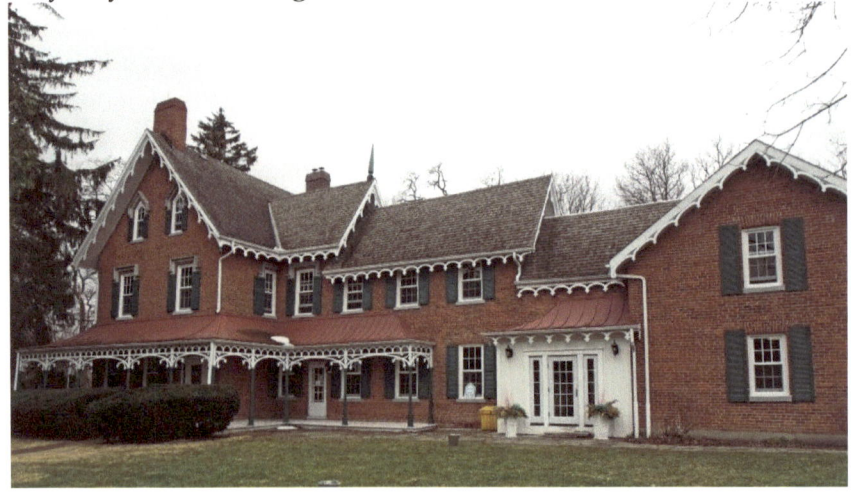

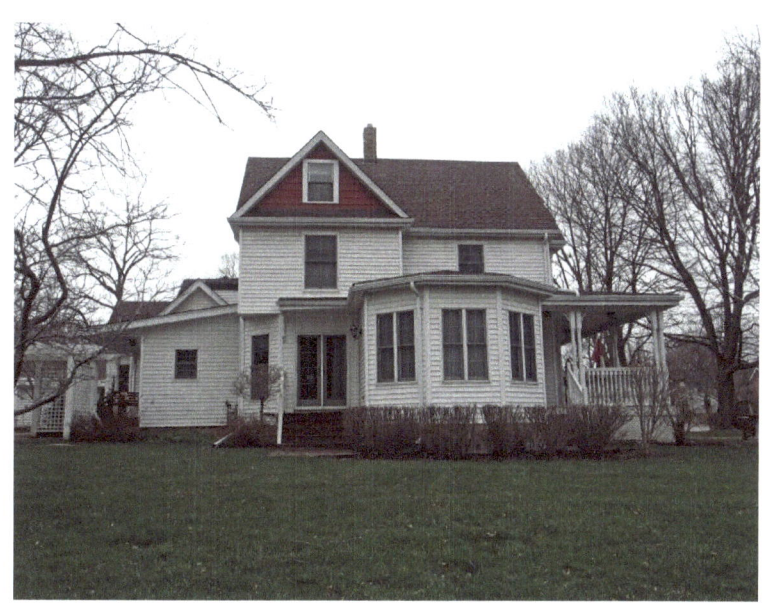

26 George Street

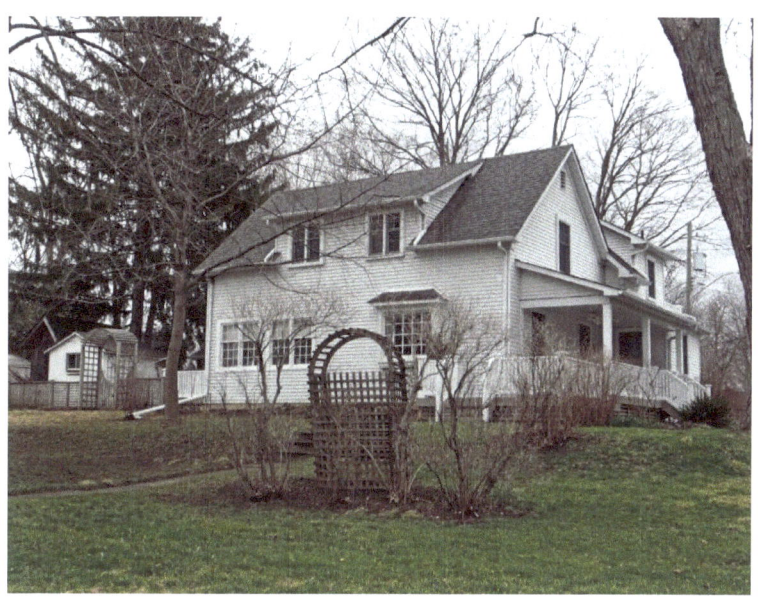

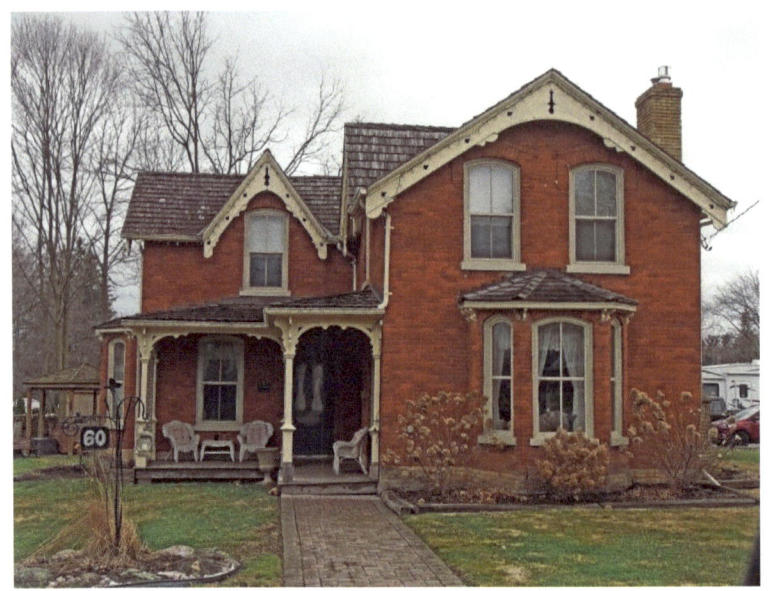

60 Queen Street – Alexander Campbell House – c. 1868

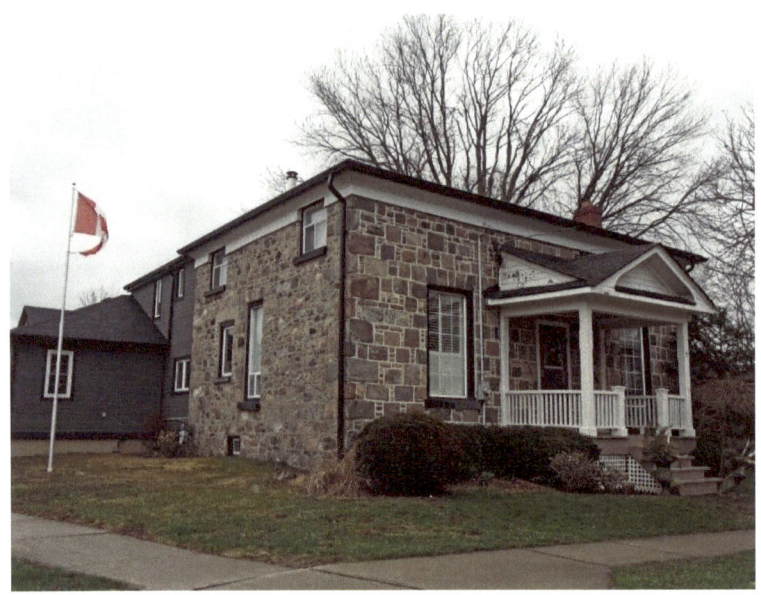

33 Duke Street – c. 1860 - This stone granite home, which has square cut building stones on the front façade (referred to as ashlar stone), was bought by James Mitchell in 1878.

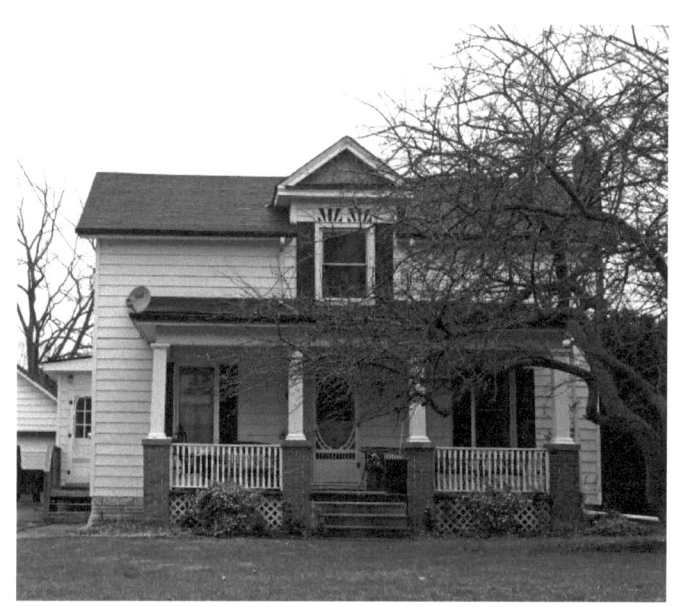

Duke Street

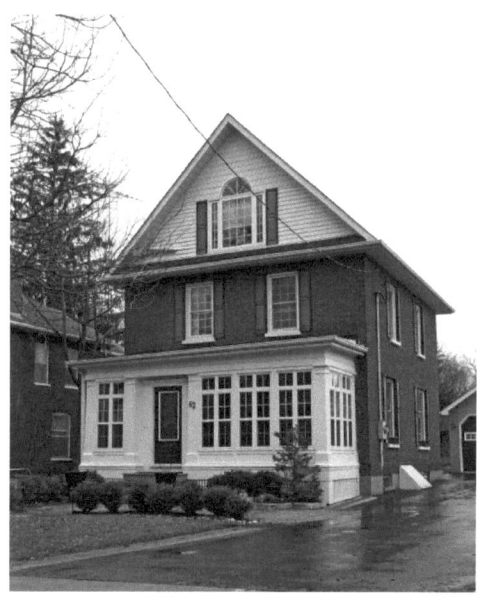

62 Duke Street

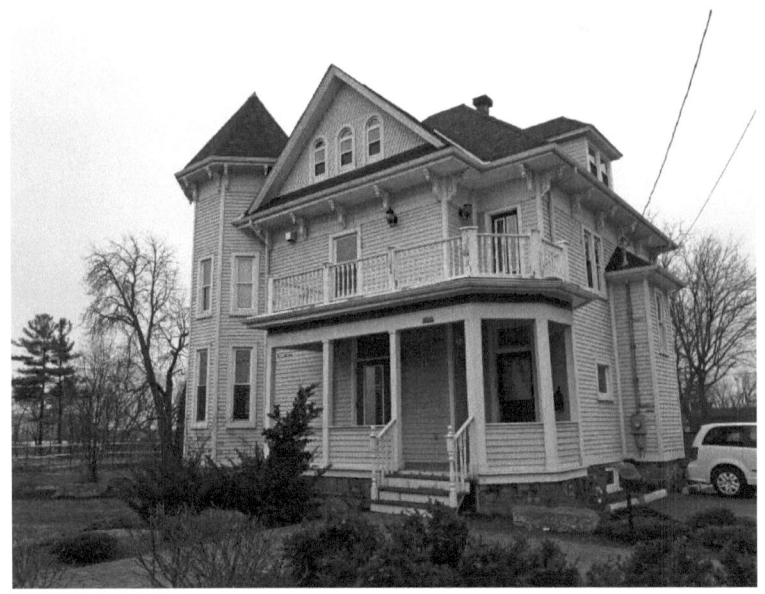

1200 Consumers Drive

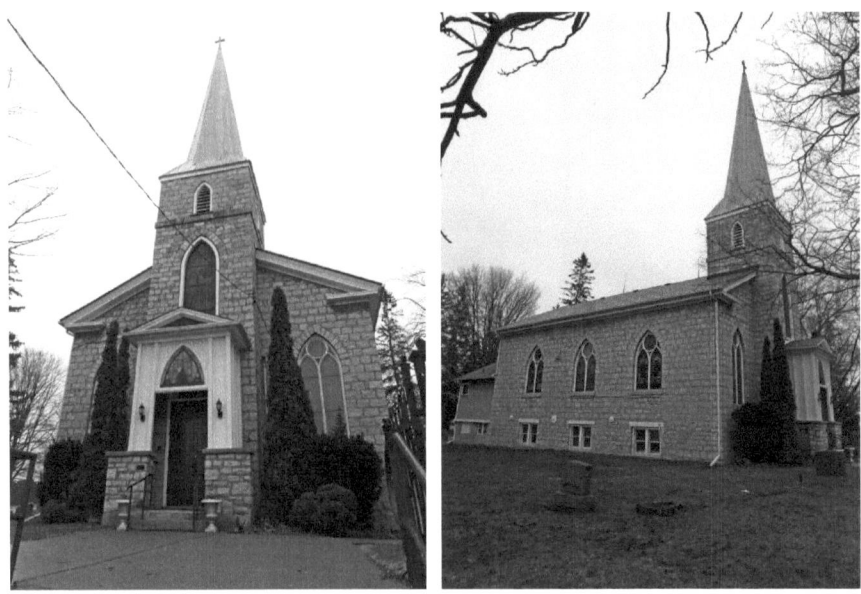

150 Victoria Street East - St. John's Anglican Church - c. 1846 –
Kingston limestone

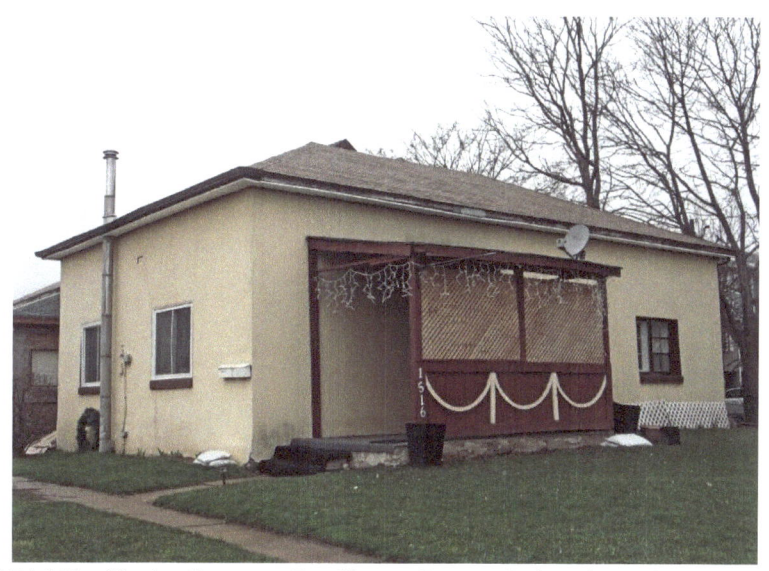

1516 Dufferin Street - Dufferin Street School c. 1851 - This brick school house was the meeting place of the County Council when Ontario County was formed in 1852. It served as a school until Brock Street School was built in 1916. It is now a private residence.

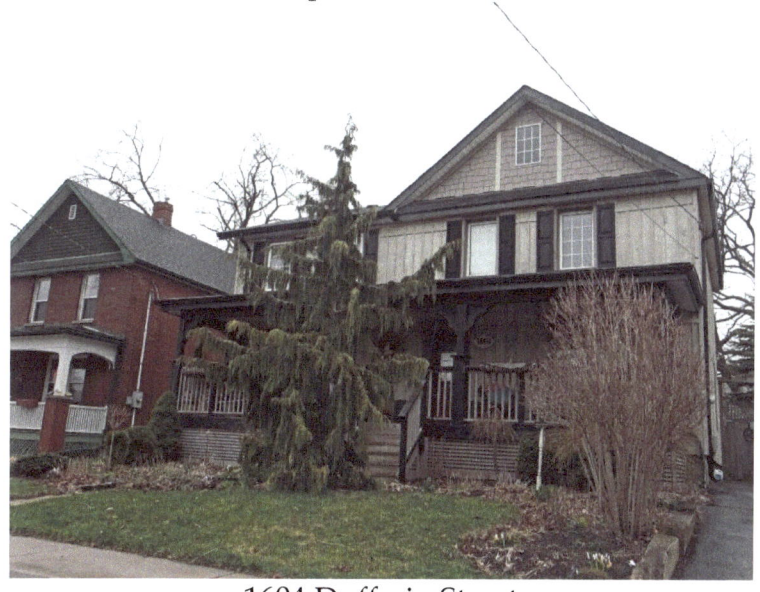

1604 Dufferin Street

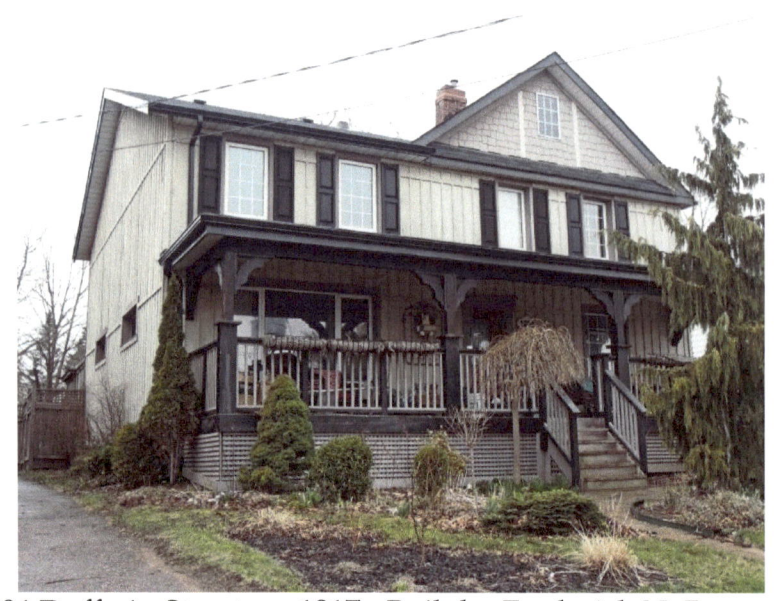

1604 Dufferin Street - c. 1917 - Built by Frederick N. Burns, an early Whitby entrepreneur, this house was purchased by St. John's Anglican Church in 1925 as a rectory.

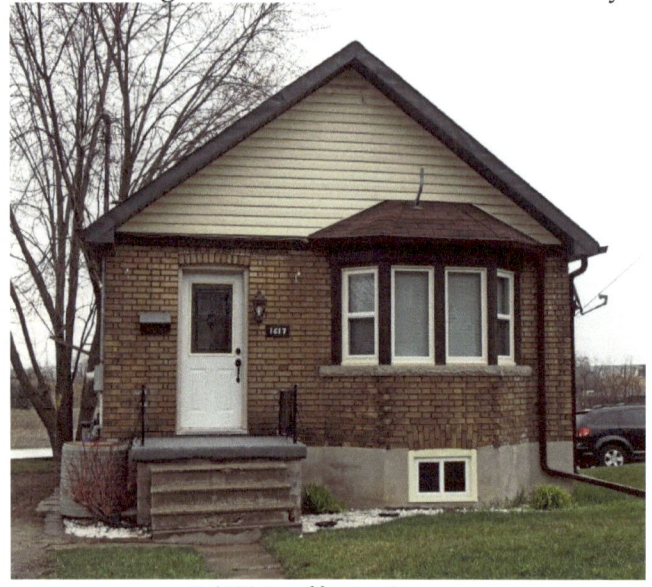

1617 Dufferin Street

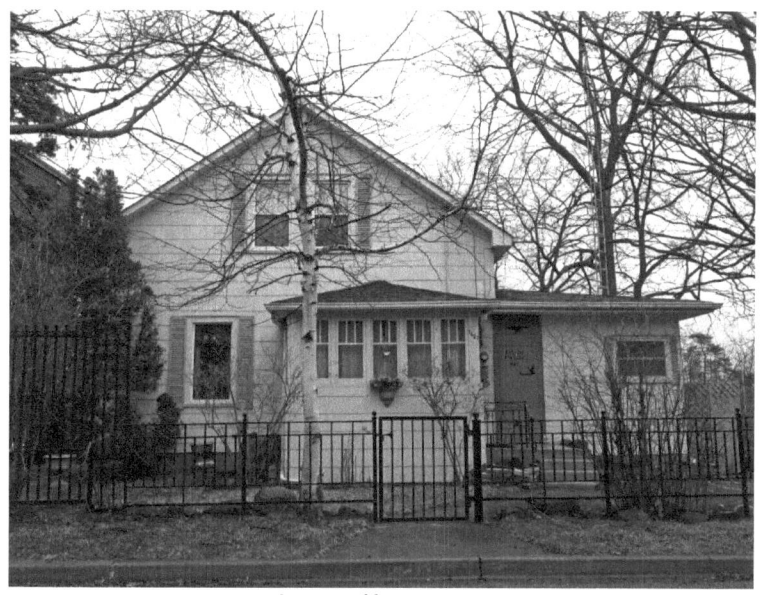

1627 Dufferin Street

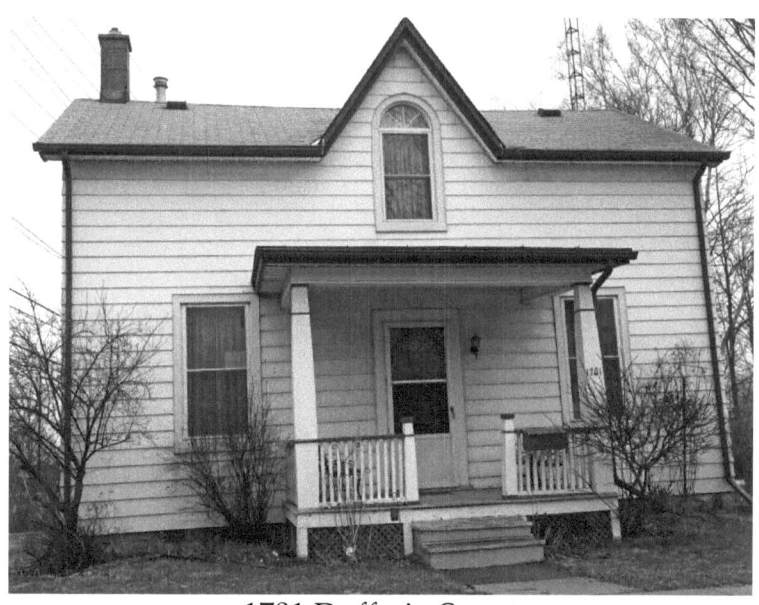

1701 Dufferin Street

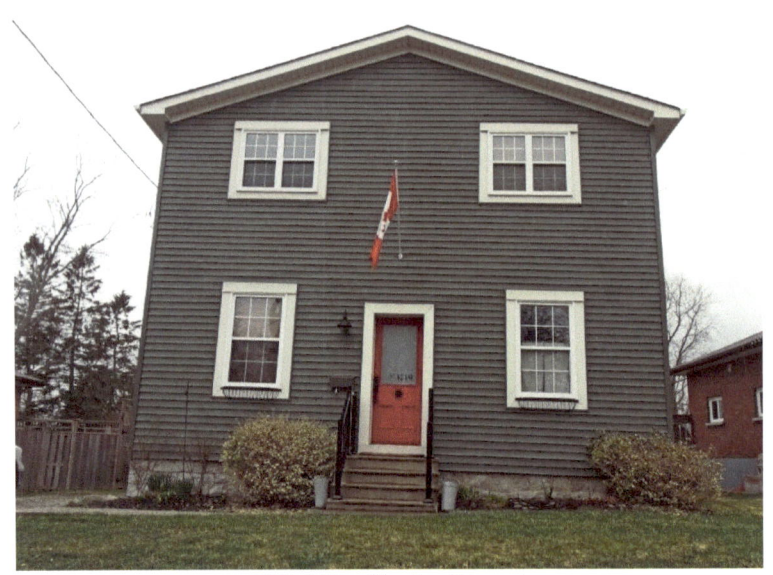

1716 Dufferin Street

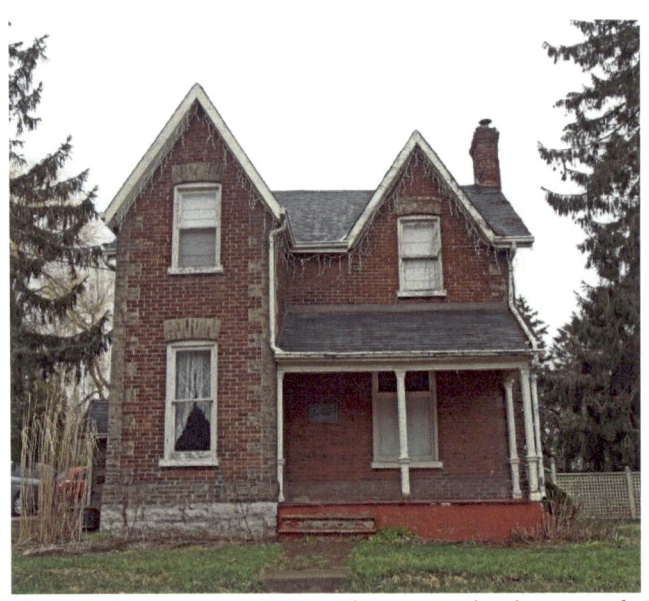

1751 Dufferin Street – c. 1893 - This was the home of Captain Richard Goldring, a sailor on Lake Ontario; later he operated a general store and post office at Port Whitby.

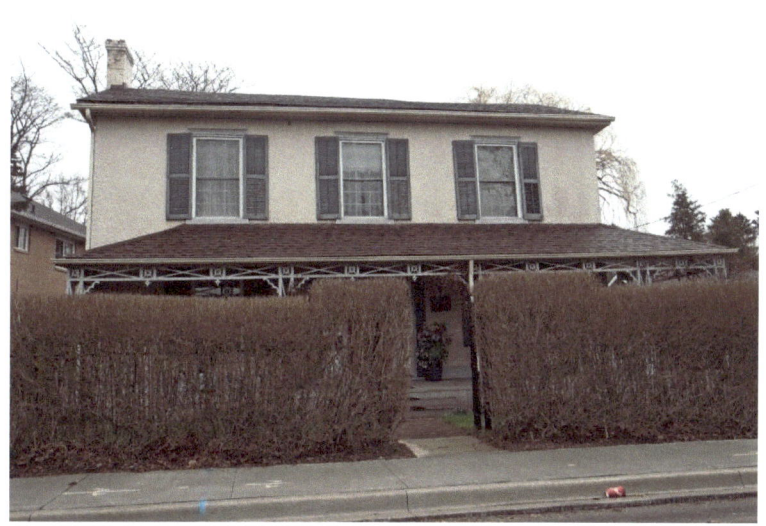

1733 Dufferin Street - Watson/Galbraith House - c. 1857 - This was the home of John Watson (1806-1879) a grain dealer at Port Whitby, and one of the first Whitby Councillors for Port Whitby, now the South Ward. Together with James Rowe, Watson helped develop the Port into a thriving community in the 1850s and 1860s. The house was later owned by David Galbraith one of the owners of Whitby Harbour who served as Harbormaster.

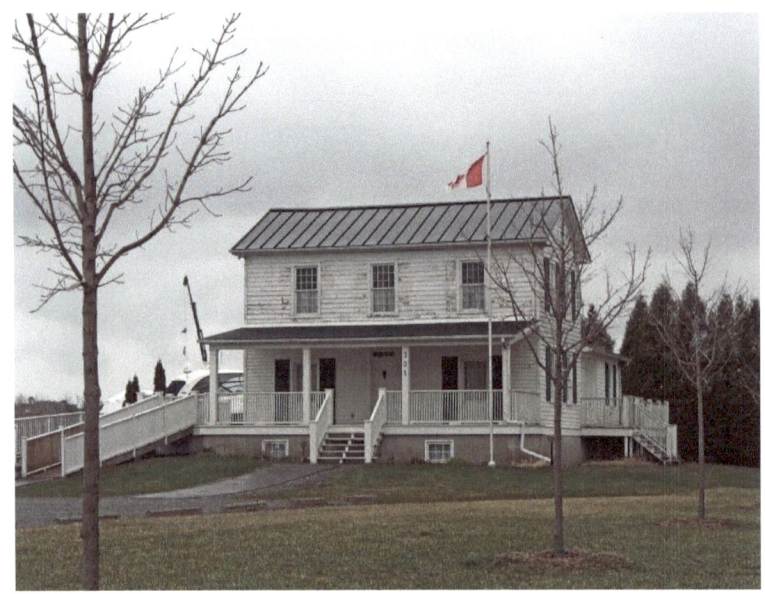

301 Front Street - c. 1856 - This frame house was built for Captain James Rowe, Whitby's first Mayor. The house contains the original interior central hall floor plan. Rowe was a prominent grain merchant who was responsible for the development of the harbour at Port Whitby. It was relocated in 1999 and is now a museum run by the Whitby Community Heritage Association.

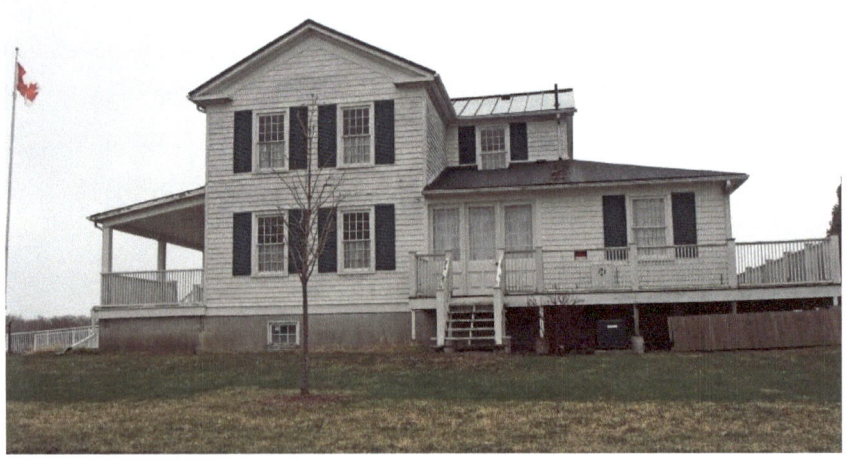

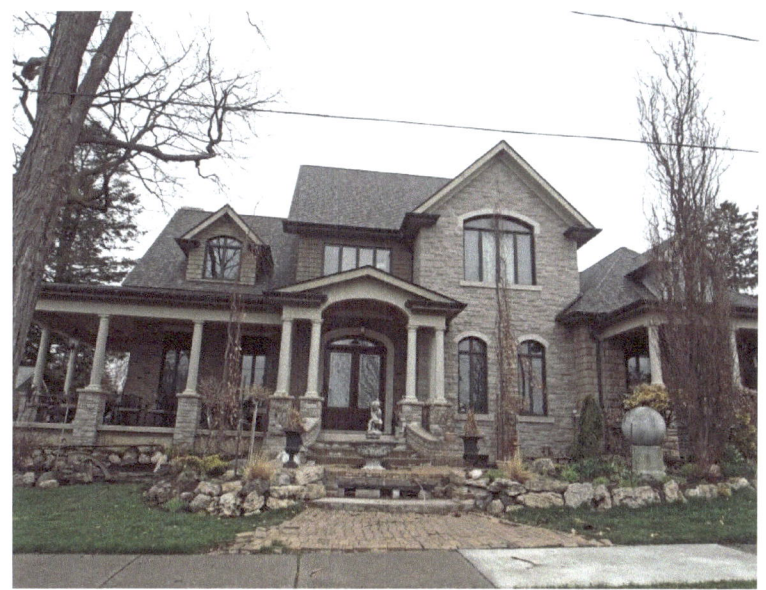

134 Front Street – c. 1910-19 - This house, owned by Captain Richard Goldring, was one of the first built in Whitby of precast concrete blocks.

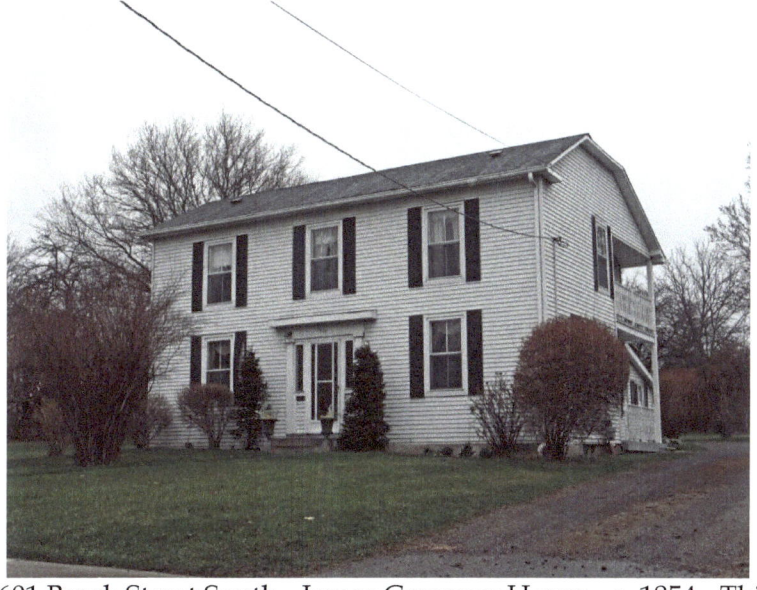

1601 Brock Street South - James Cameron House - c. 1854 - This house was built for James Cameron, a retired farmer who settled on the site of the Ontario Hospital lands in 1831.

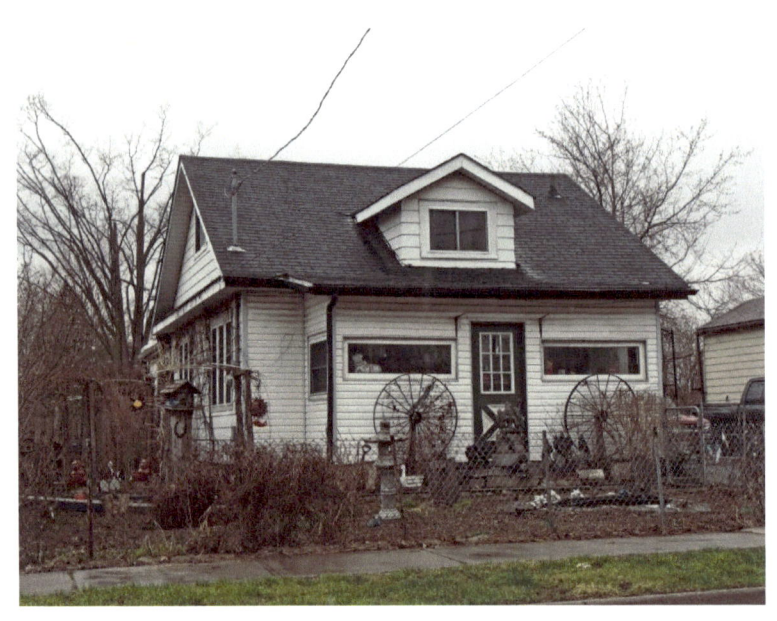

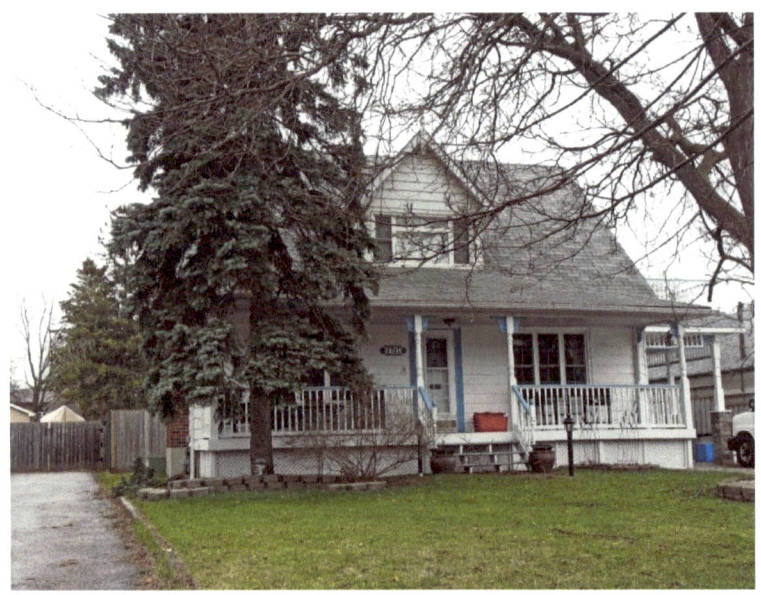

#1721

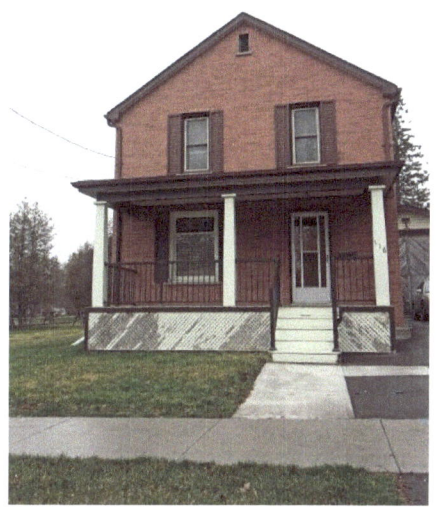

116 Watson Street West

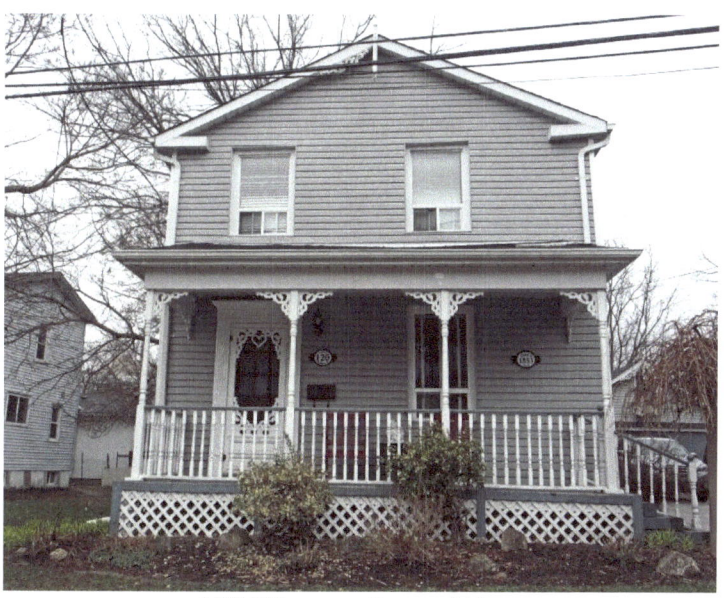

120 Watson Street West

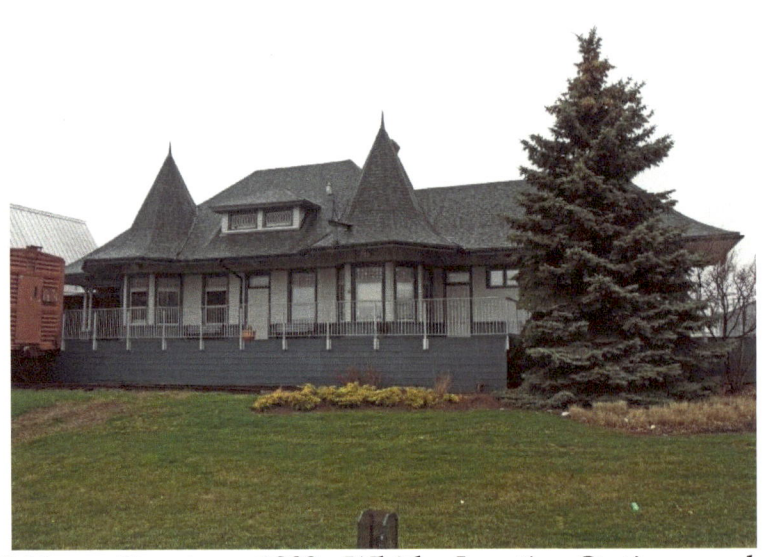

1450 Henry Street – c. 1903 - Whitby Junction Station was built at the foot of Byron Street for the Grand Trunk Railway (GTR) in 1903. Its turrets and bays were typical of train stations along the GTR because they provided functional elements needed for telegraph operators to view incoming and outgoing trains. The low-hanging roof offered protection to passengers on the platforms. The station's low and linear design layout is reminiscent of the Arts and Crafts style, the elements of which serve to blend and enhance the relationship between the landscape and architecture; the station's many windows served to help bring the outside in. In 1970 the station was adapted into an art gallery.

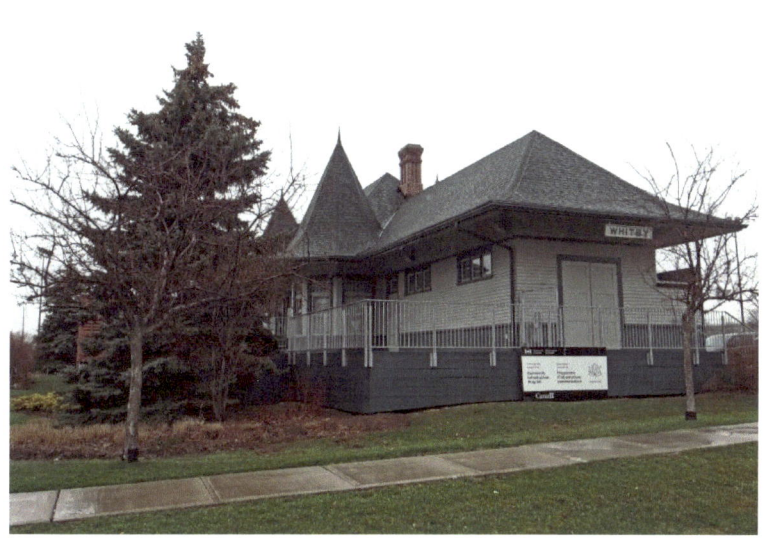

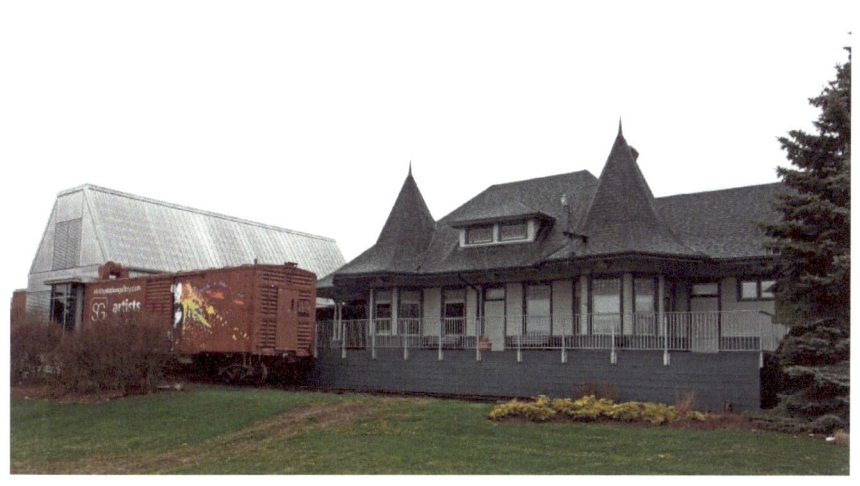

www.ingramcontent.com/pod-product-compliance
Lightning Source LLC
Chambersburg PA
CBHW040242220526
45473CB00001B/343